Peace, Love & Blessings,
Monie

PRAYING FOR OUR FAMILIES *from* PASSOVER TO PENTECOST

50 Days of Prayer

By
MONIE BROADUS

Praying for our Families from Passover to Pentecost: 50 Days of Prayer

by Monie Broadus

Printed in the United States of America

Scripture quotations marked KJV are from the King James Version of the Bible. Scripture quotations marked NIV are from the New International Version. Scripture quotations marked AMP are from the Amplified version of the Holy Bible. Scripture quotations marked ESV are from the English Standard Version.

Cover design and graphic designs by Andrea Haynes

Photography by Jessica Broadus

Dedication

This book is dedicated to my Lord and Savior, Jesus Christ who is the lover of my soul. He feeds me daily with spiritual meat and bread and inspires and encourages me so that I am energized to encourage others. He blessed me to move away from scripted prayers of repetition and taught me how to converse with Him and pray in the spirit. Without Him I am lost, but with Him I can do all things, for He is my strength.

Appreciations

My greatest earthly encourager and biggest cheerleader has been my Dad George who went home to be with my Lord, May 17, 2012. I thank God for the instructions from George and my mother, Myrtle who reared all 10 children in the admonition of the Lord.

A special thanks to my husband, Bernard, whom I honor and love, my daughters, Jasmine, Jessica and Angelica, my son, Robert, my son-in-laws, Eric and DeJesus and Grandma's babies, Amayah, Lauryn and DeJesus, Jr. Also, I want to thank my friends Denise Sutton for editing and Sharon Bell Hudson for her inspiration.

Lastly, a special thanks to my spiritual mother and Pastor, Apostle Brenda Medley, all the missionaries of Empowered Ministries, Inc. and all my wonderful prayer warring partners.

Explanation of Punctuation

All references to my Lord and Savior, Jesus Christ within my writings in this book are capitalized in honor of God's Supremacy, Greatness and Majesty.

INTRODUCTION

Prayer is our conversation with God. It's a powerful tool that can move mountains, but many people even Christians only use it when a crisis arises. I've been blessed to be part of a ministry where we have been taught the power of prayer and also fasting. My pastor, Apostle Brenda Medley at Empowered Ministries, Inc. (EMI) in Landover, Maryland has also challenged us to get into the presence of God and pray prayers that would move the heart of God. Our EMI Missionary Board over the last several years has completed many 21-day corporate fasts as well as fasted as a group and fasted individually. It's been enjoyable and very rewarding especially as God has called us up higher and blessed us with spiritual and natural gifts, healing and insight. With all the wonderful benefits that I personally have enjoyed from fasting and praying, I'm always encouraging others to enjoy and partake of God's great banquet. Fasting is eating in the spirit, for God is our spiritual food and nourishment. He is a rewarder of those who diligently seek Him (Hebrews 11:6). So I asked myself this question; "Why wouldn't everyone want to fast and pray?" Many want the rewards and benefits without the additional sacrifice. God indicated that there are many people who will not fast with you, but they will pray with you, encourage them to pray. From that conversation with God, the original 50 Days of Prayer was birthed.

With all the obligations to ministry, family and work, I wondered how we (EMI Missionaries) would be able to pray together for 50 days. Are you familiar with the phrase, *Keep it simple*? God led us to take the simple route, use the EMI prayer line. We invited family, friends and many who were not members of our church to join us in prayer daily on our prayer line. A good friend, Dana Randolph couldn't pray with us in the mornings. Our 7:00 a.m. EST calls were too early for Dana, who is on CST, but she shared with two friends, Brenda in St. Louis and Natasha in New Orleans and our numbers of prayer warriors increased immediately. So we journeyed through *50 Days of Prayer: Praying From Passover to Pentecost*. It was such a blessing that God inspired me to encourage us to do it again, this time specifically just for our families. Part II became *50 Days of Prayer: Praying For Our Families.* That was in the fall of 2012. Now we have set aside that special period from Passover to Pentecost as our annual 50 days of prayer for our families.

The prayer line has grown and so have we. Today we are sharing our prayer journal with you and invite you to pray along with us in 2014. Our 50 days will encompass Passover through Pentecost and we are again praying for our families (April 20 through June 8). Our prayer line number is 1.712.775.7000 and the code is 323604#. Dial in during this period Sundays – Fridays at 7:00 am EST and on Saturdays at 8:30 am EST. Additionally, we will be calling in on Wednesday evenings at 7:30 pm EST.

To all those churches, ministries, and individuals who will use this prayer guide to pray for your families, be led by the Spirit of God to move in intercession as the Holy Spirit guides you. God will give you other scriptures and numerous examples to use as you teach and as you pray. Have a listening ear for God's voice as you intercede, then pray what you hear. God is well able to pull down any stronghold, His arms are not too short, neither is anything too hard for Him. Trust and believe and He shall bring change and deliverance in your family and He's going to use you to do it.

May God add special blessing to everyone who will be inspired to pray the prayers in this journal and intercede on behalf of their families, friends and love ones.

-Monie Broadus

CONTENTS

50 Days of PRAYER

Praying for our Families from Passover to Pentecost

by Monie Broadus

GOD'S FAMILY

The Family

A family is a social unit which may include parents and children, a husband and a wife, sisters and brothers, aunts, uncles and cousins, including in-laws, step children and step parents. They may all live together or in separate dwellings. The family will function well together when they reside in unity, however when there is disharmony and disunity they may be labeled as dysfunctional and may experience much discord and conflict. We are familiar with traditional family units and even those which are classified as dysfunctional. On our first day we are going to repent of our sins and the sins of our families. Afterwards on day 2 we will be praying for God's Family, which is the kingdom of God.

DAY 1 – A DAY OF ATONEMENT

In the lives of the Jewish people the Day of Atonement is the holiest and most solemn day of the year. As we begin our 50 days of prayer, let's make today our day to atone for the sins of our families and our love ones, including our ancestors. Let us ask God to help us to amend our own behavior and seek forgiveness for our sins and the sins of our family. No matter whether we have been right or wrong in situations with our spouses, parents and children, let us on purpose forgive and move forward. Bless peace to be restored and our families healed, make a fresh start on a new day and walk in victory. Then, ask God to forgive our families of wrong doing. Job gives us a good example of a father covering his children just in case they sinned. **Job 1:5** And it was so, when the days of their feasting were gone about, that Job sent and sanctified them, and rose up early in the morning, and offered burnt offerings according to the number of them all: for Job said, It may be that my sons have sinned, and cursed God in their hearts. Thus did Job continually (KJV). The Day of Atonement is all about forgiveness. Let's ask God to help us get better and not bitter, to drop the ball and chain that we have been carrying around and be blessed with every chain and shackle broken, delivered, healed and set free.

> **Leviticus 23:26-28** [26] And the Lord spake unto Moses, saying, 27 Also on the tenth day of this seventh month there shall be a day of atonement: it shall be an holy convocation unto you; and ye shall afflict your souls, and offer an offering made by fire unto the Lord. 28 And ye shall do no work in that same day: for it is a day of atonement, to make an atonement for you before the Lord your God (KJV).

Prayer

Heavenly Father, in the name of Jesus, I bless Your name and give you glory. You are a kind and forgiving Lord, You are my Redeemer and my Saving Grace. Bless Your sweet, holy, honorable, majestic and matchless name. I give glory to You my King, my Waymaker, my Strong Tower, my present Help in the times of trouble. You are the Lord who cares for me and You care about all of Your children. Today I come before You to be cleansed. I ask for Your forgiveness of all my sins, confessed and un-confessed, those I committed willingly and those I committed unknowingly. I repent of all my transgressions and my iniquities and ask You to cleanse me from the inside out. Remove hatred, envy and strife from my heart and fill it with love, peace and joy that I may spread it abundantly throughout my family for generations to come, in Jesus name. Lord I repent also for my internal and external family, my children, the generations before me and those that shall come afterwards, forgive all of their missteps, their mistreatments of others, their unforgiving hearts and their unlovely ways. Bless us all with clean and contrite hearts and give us a servant's heart in Jesus name. Lord bless us all to get better and not bitter, to let go of every weight that we have carried and be blessed with every chain and shackle broken and every yoke of bondage destroyed. Deliver, heal and set us free, in Jesus name, I pray, Amen.

DAY 2 – WHO IS GOD'S FAMILY? THE FAMILY OF JESUS

Jesus identifies those who will do the will of the Father as His brother, His sister and His mother. So those who do the will of the Father are His family. The world didn't know Him and it does not know us. Those who believe in Him continue to change, repent of their sins and stop sinning habitually, for a seed of righteousness has been planted in them. The children of God exhibit His character, they show love towards their brothers and sisters and do what is right. Those who do not do what is right and do not love their brothers and sisters are following the ways of the devil. They shall be known by their fruit.

Mark 3:31-35 [31]There came then his brethren and his mother, and, standing without, sent unto him, calling him. [32] And the multitude sat about him, and they said unto him, Behold, thy mother and thy brethren without seek for thee. [33] And he answered them, saying, Who is my mother, or my brethren? [34] And he looked round about on them which sat about him, and said, Behold my mother and my brethren! [35] For whosoever shall do the will of God, the same is my brother, and my sister, and mother (KJV).

Prayer

Abba, our Father, Creator of Heaven and Earth, in the name of Jesus, I thank You for being the Savior of my soul. You're a great and mighty God and You are greatly to be praised. From the rising of the sun until the going down of the same, You are worthy Lord of all honor, glory and praise. You are the King of all kings and the Lord of all lords and matchless is all Your ways, bless Your sweet holy, honorable and adorable name. You created us all and are the Lord of all.

You have called us to be one, united together on one accord as one family, Your family. You have made us joint heirs with Jesus Christ and called us into Your Kingdom and into Your family. Forgive us Lord of all of our sins, make us new and cleanse us from the crown of our heads to the soles of our feet. Give us clean hands and a clean heart that we might serve You. As peculiar people and priests and members of Your royal priesthood, thank You for blessing us to join Your family and enter Your Kingdom. Bless us to be discerning and wise in all our ways. Use us Lord to bring those family members who have strayed away like lost lambs back into the sheepfold and bless them Lord that they be saved. Use us like magnets to draw our brothers and sisters who are lost into Your family, which is the Kingdom of God, in Jesus name, Amen.

DAY 3 – THE BODY OF CHRIST

We are all one big family in the Body of Christ and God has called us to be unified together on one accord to carry out the Great Co-Mission, Jesus with us saving souls. **Mark 16:15** And he said unto them, Go ye into all the world, and preach the gospel to every creature (KJV). When we work together as one, we're unmovable, unshakable and unstoppable!

> **Ephesians 4:1-6** [1]I therefore, the prisoner of the Lord, beseech you that ye walk worthy of the vocation wherewith ye are called, [2]With all lowliness and meekness, with longsuffering, forbearing one another in love; [3]Endeavouring to keep the unity of the Spirit in the bond of peace. [4]There is one body, and one Spirit, even as ye are called in one hope of your calling; [5]One Lord, one faith, one baptism, [6]One God and Father of all, who is above all, and through all, and in you all (KJV).

Prayer

Lord God Almighty, the One who is the Alpha and the Omega, the Rock of Ages, the One and only Living God, Lord we magnify You, we lift You up on high and we give Your name glory. You are our soon and coming King. In Jesus name, we offer You thanksgiving and praise for You are the Lover of our souls, our Burden Bearer and our Place of Refuge. Lord forgive us for sowing seeds of discord in our own family, the Body of Christ. Forgive us for placing more weight in doctrines verses coming together on one accord in agreement with the death, burial and resurrection of Jesus Christ who brought us salvation and saved our souls. Bless us to let go of our differences and embrace the truth for the blood of Jesus cleanses all. Help us to live lives that are transformed and holy and acceptable unto You. Forgive our sins and restore our souls. Lord we ask You to smear the Body of Christ with Your anointing with Your fresh oil for the journey. Have mercy upon all our spiritual mothers, fathers and leaders, bless the Body of Christ to walk together in agreement, in Jesus name we pray, Amen.

DAY 4 – THE 5-FOLD MINISTRY

In the Body of Christ, God purposed specific work for the 5-Fold Ministry. He is still calling the 5-Fold Ministry today for the perfecting of the saints, for the work of the ministry, and for the edifying of the body of Christ. The work has not changed over time, it yet remains the same. So we should give no place to pride or haughty thoughts exalting ourselves above others, and not think too highly of ourselves. The same One who has raised us up from our humble circumstances and gifted us with His anointing has need of us to work in concert, in harmony with like minds and like spirits until He returns.

> **Ephesians 4:1-6 (see day 3) 7-12, 13-16** [7]But unto every one of us is given grace according to the measure of the gift of Christ. [8]Wherefore he saith, When he ascended up on high, he led captivity captive, and gave gifts unto men. [9](Now that he ascended, what is it but that he also descended first into the lower parts of the earth? [10]He that descended is the same also that ascended up far above all heavens, that he might fill all things.) [11]And he gave some, apostles; and some, prophets; and some, evangelists; and some, pastors and teachers; [12]**For the perfecting of the saints, for the work of the ministry, for the edifying of the body of Christ:**

[13]Till we all come in the unity of the faith, and of the knowledge of the Son of God, unto a perfect man, unto the measure of the stature of the fullness of Christ: [14]That we henceforth be no more children, tossed to and fro, and carried about with every wind of doctrine, by the sleight of men, and cunning craftiness, whereby they lie in wait to deceive; [15]But speaking the truth in love, may grow up into him in all things, which is the head, even Christ: [16]From whom the whole body fitly joined together and compacted by that which every joint supplieth, according to the effectual working in the measure of every part, maketh increase of the body unto the edifying of itself in love (KJV).

Prayer

Father God you have called the 5-Fold Ministry to perform specific work for You for the perfecting of the saints until Your return. In Jesus name Lord bless the 5-Fold Ministry to walk together in agreement with like minds and like spirits, doing great and mighty works on Your behalf to bring You glory. Lord we bind up all discord and competitive spirits right now within the 5- Fold Ministry in the name of Jesus and command them to dry up and we cast them into the sea, in Jesus name. We lose the spirit of unity and oneness and speak the blessing of the Lord over the Body of Christ, in Jesus name, Amen.

DAY 5 – HEIRS TO THE THRONE: SONS OF GOD

When we come into the kingdom of God, as a believer we are adopted into the family of God and are all sons of God. We now have a new and different relationship with God. As an adopted person we gain full rights to our Father's estate. Our new privileges include no longer being led by fear, but rather being led by the Spirit of the One and only Living God. We are joint heirs with Jesus Christ. It is not by accident or happen stance that we become heirs along with Jesus. In fact, this was His plan from the beginning.

Roman 8:14-17 [14] For as many as are led by the Spirit of God, these are sons of God. [15] For you did not receive the spirit of bondage again to fear, but you received the Spirit of adoption by whom we cry out, "Abba, Father." [16] The Spirit itself beareth witness with our spirit, that we are the children of God: [17] And if children, then heirs; heirs of God, and joint-heirs with Christ; if so be that we suffer with him, that we may be also glorified together (KJV).

Galatians 4:5-6 [5] to redeem those who were under the law, that we might receive the adoption as sons. 6 And because you are sons, God has sent forth the Spirit of His Son into your hearts, crying, "Abba, Father (KJV)!"

Ephesians 1:5 he predestined us for adoption to sonship through Jesus Christ, in accordance with his pleasure and will— (NIV)

Prayer

Abba, Our Father, in the name of Jesus, we bless our Lord Jesus who has made us joint heirs and sons of God. His death, burial and resurrection made it possible for us to be a part of Your family. Lord we thank You for receiving us as sons when we repent and accept Jesus as our Redeemer and our Savior. Bless and use us God to draw others into Your Family. Use us Lord to bring our brothers and sisters into Your Kingdom, for You have taught us that those who do Your will are Your family (Mark 3:31-35), in Jesus name we pray, Amen.

DAY 6 – ENCOURAGING YOUR BROTHER

Make sure to let those who are your pastors, spiritual leaders and elders know how much you appreciate them. Articulate how their leadership and teaching, helped you to grow and mature. Remember they make great sacrifices for the ministry and labor before the Lord in prayer on your behalf. God expects us to lift one another up, to encourage each other. In fact, He has even called us to assemble together to encourage and strengthen one another, to share our faith and our testimonies. Some of us today believe in God, but we skip the assembling together of the saints. God has a specific purpose for us attending church, don't stay home and miss your blessings. Your story of deliverance is just what someone else needs to hear to be encouraged to wait on the Lord until their breakthrough comes.

If you're in the presence of someone who has anxiety or is depressed, bless them with an encouraging word. Sometimes they just need a listening ear, a comforting hug, someone to touch or hold their hand. You may lead them in prayer or sing a song. Be sensitive to the Holy Spirit, He will lead you and guide you. It may be that only your presence is required, listen for God's voice and respond accordingly. Remember, you are your brother's keeper.

1 Thessalonians 5:11-16 [11] Wherefore comfort yourselves together, and edify one another, even as also ye do. [12] And we beseech you, brethren, to know them which labour among you, and are over you in the Lord, and admonish you; [13] And to esteem them very highly in love for their work's sake. And be at peace among yourselves. [14] Now we exhort you, brethren, warn them that are unruly, comfort the feebleminded, support the weak, be patient toward all men. [15] See that none render evil for evil unto any man; but ever follow that which is good, both among yourselves, and to all men. [16] Rejoice evermore (KJV).

Philippians 4:8 [8] Finally, brethren, whatsoever things are true, whatsoever things are honest, whatsoever things are just, whatsoever things are pure, whatsoever things are lovely, whatsoever things are of good report; if there be any virtue, and if there be any praise, think on these things (KJV).

Hebrews 10:25 [25] Not forsaking the assembling of ourselves together, as the manner of some is; but exhorting one another: and so much the more, as ye see the day approaching (KJV).

Prayer

Heavenly Father, in the name of Jesus, I thank You Lord for encouraging my soul. Thank You for lifting my heavy burdens and lifting my head. Thank You for destroying yokes of bondage, breaking shackles and chains and for blessing my spirit and making me whole. Bless me to share my experience of how You have encouraged me and kept me through trials and tribulation. Use me to lift and encourage my brothers. Let the shared experiences of my life bless someone else to take the roads and the paths that lead directly to You. Thank You for being longsuffering with me and help me to be longsuffering with my brothers, in Jesus name I pray, Amen.

DAY 7 – PRAYING FOR OUR SPIRITUAL FATHERS

The Apostle Paul was Timothy's spiritual father. He taught him and others just as he would a biological son and brought them up in the ways of the Lord. He was like a shepherd to them as many of our pastors, elders and church leaders are for us. The Apostle John addresses the followers of Jesus Christ as little children, in 1John 2:1, 12, 13, 18 and 28. He uses little children as an endearing term as a father would to his own children. Let us petition the Lord today on behalf of our spiritual fathers.

1 Corinthians 4:14-17 [14] I write not these things to shame you, but as my beloved sons I warn you. [15] For though ye have ten thousand instructers in Christ, yet have ye not many fathers: for in Christ Jesus I have begotten you through the gospel. [16] Wherefore I beseech you, be ye followers of me. [17] For this cause have I sent unto you Timotheus, who is my beloved son, and faithful in the Lord, who shall bring you into remembrance of my ways which be in Christ, as I teach every where in every church (KJV).

Prayer

Holy Father, God of Power and Might, in the name of Your Son Jesus, bless Your glorious and victorious name. Thank you for blessing us with faithful men of God, mighty men of valor whom You have raised up who are more than mentors, they are our spiritual fathers. Use us Lord to bless them for You by giving of our time, talents and resources. Thank You for using them to pour into our lives. Jehovah Jireh, provide all of their needs, mentally, spiritually, physically

and emotionally and financially. Bless their ministries, marriages, families and their homes. We pray that they experience Your power through Your Spirit in their preaching, teaching, healing and deliverance. Bless them with a discerning spirit, give them a kind and understanding heart. Make them wise counselors, who counsel Your children with the wisdom of Christ, Our Lord and Savior. Lord, give them oneness in mind with Jesus Christ and increase their anointing to destroy yokes of bondage like never before. Lord use them for Your glory, in Jesus name we pray, Amen.

DAY 8 – PRAYING FOR OUR SPIRITUAL MOTHERS

One biblical account in the word regarding a relationship between a mother-in-law and a daughter-in-law, I am using today to talk about spiritual mothers. Just the words in the scriptures in Ruth 1:16-17 demonstrate the admiration, respect and love that Ruth had towards Naomi. Naomi had such an impact on Ruth's life that even after the death of her spouse, Ruth willingly on her own accord follows Naomi and leaves her native country and her birth family for a life without idol worship, but worship of the one and only living God. It reminds me of how powerful the influence of our spiritual mothers, those women who are pastors, preachers, teachers and apostles, like Paul are in our lives. Lord we thank and bless You for them. (There is more about Ruth and Naomi on Day 37 - In-laws).

> **Ruth 1:16-17** [16] And Ruth said, Entreat me not to leave thee, or to return from following after thee: for whither thou goest, I will go; and where thou lodgest, I will lodge: thy people shall be my people, and thy God my God: [17] Where thou diest, will I die, and there will I be buried: the LORD do so to me, and more also, if ought but death part thee and me (KJV).

Prayer

My dear Heavenly Father, in the name of Jesus, I bless, thank and give You praise for my spiritual mother. Bless You Lord for allowing me to serve You by aiding her in ministry. You have blessed her to be a good Shepherd and a wise ruler who is due double honor. Lord I ask that You protect her from all spiritual enemies and all hurt and harm. I bind up all distractions and hindrances to the mission that You have called her to and lose them to dry places. Father strengthen her, cause her to prosper and grow, bless her with divine health, increase her finances and enlarge her territory. Bless her Lord with Your peace and Your joy. Increase Your power in the gifts You have given her and increase Your anointing in her life through Your Spirit in Jesus name, I pray, Amen.

DAY 9 – PRAYING FOR GOD'S KINGDOM TO COME

Jesus is our soon and coming King, you don't have to look far to see the birth pains of the Earth. There are wars and rumors of wars. The unrest in Syria and other nations is no longer shocking and surprising. There have been all types of storms and earthquakes. Katrina devastated New Orleans and Sandy brought havoc on the northeastern coast in New Jersey and New York, an area hardly ever hit by hurricanes. Australia has had flooding, Tsunamis have hit Japan and Typhoon Haiyan just hit the Philippines. Weekly there are gunmen in malls, work places, schools and airports where the ages of those going postal are younger and younger. Many of the perpetrators have mental issues, are lost and live a life of misery. They don't seem to know where to turn and are often suicidal. Same sex marriages are being blessed and laws are being passed to support them. God You said in Your word that man lying with a man as he does naturally with a woman is an abomination. We should all pay attention to the times in which we live. Lord help us redeem the times for the days are evil. Night comes and no man can work (Ephesians 5:16, John 9:4).

When Jesus comes back as He has promised, every knee is going to bow and every tongue is going to confess that He is Lord (Philippians 2:10). In His second coming, He will reign over all. All evil will be destroyed and He will establish the new heaven and the new earth (Revelation 21:1). There will be no more sorrow, sickness, disease, death or pain. He won the victory at Calvary and He is coming back for His family. As He is preparing a place for us, let us go out into the fields which are ripe to bring many into the family, especially those who are spiritually weak and those who are lost, Amen.

Matthew 6:7-13 [7] But when ye pray, use not vain repetitions, as the heathen do: for they think that they shall be heard for their much speaking. [8] Be not ye therefore like unto them: for your Father knoweth what things ye have need of, before ye ask him. [9] After this manner therefore pray ye: Our Father which art in heaven, Hallowed be thy name. [10] Thy kingdom come, Thy will be done in earth, as it is in heaven. [11] Give us this day our daily bread. [12] And forgive us our debts, as we forgive our debtors. [13] And lead us not into temptation, but deliver us from evil: For thine is the kingdom, and the power, and the glory, for ever. Amen (KJV).

Luke 21:27 [27] And then shall they see the Son of man coming in a cloud with power and great glory (KJV).

John 14:1-3 [1] Let not your heart be troubled: ye believe in God, believe also in me. [2] In my Father's house are many mansions: if it were not so, I would have told you. I go to prepare a place for you. [3] And if I go and prepare a place for you, I will come again, and receive you unto myself; that where I am, there ye may be also (KJV).

Revelation 1:7 [7] Behold, he cometh with clouds; and every eye shall see him, and they also which pierced him: and all kindreds of the earth shall wail because of him. Even so, Amen (KJV).

Prayer

EL Shaddai, Lord God Almighty, Elohim, Creator of Heaven and of Earth, in the name of Jesus, Lord, You are worthy of all honor, glory and praise. You are the Lord of the Harvest, our Soon and Coming King. You are the King of Glory and we bless Your name. Father forgive us for procrastinating and being disobedient to Your call to go out and compel men to come unto You, forgive all of our sins, in Jesus name. Lord bless us in this great co-mission, Christ with us saving souls. Lord You said that the harvest is plentiful, but the laborers are few (Matthew 9:37). Bless us to be soul harvesters for the kingdom of God. Save the lost Lord, draw them out of dark places into Your marvelous light. Help us Lord to redeem the times for the days are evil. Raise up more intercessors and those who will stay on the wall until Your children who are called by Your name, humble themselves and pray and seek Your face (2 Chronicles 7:14). Then You will hear from heaven, forgive their sins and heal their lands. Lord Jesus send more missionaries to distant and foreign lands, that the gospel of peace be preached to every creature, in Jesus name. Father bless Your kingdom to come and Your will to be done on earth as it is in Heaven, in Jesus name, we pray, Amen. To God be the glory!

PRAYER TARGETS AND PERSONAL NOTES

_____

_____

_____

_____

_____

_____

_____

_____

_____

_____

_____

_____

_____

_____

_____

_____

_____

_____

_____

_____

_____

_____

_____

_____

_____

_____

_____

_____

_____

_____

_____

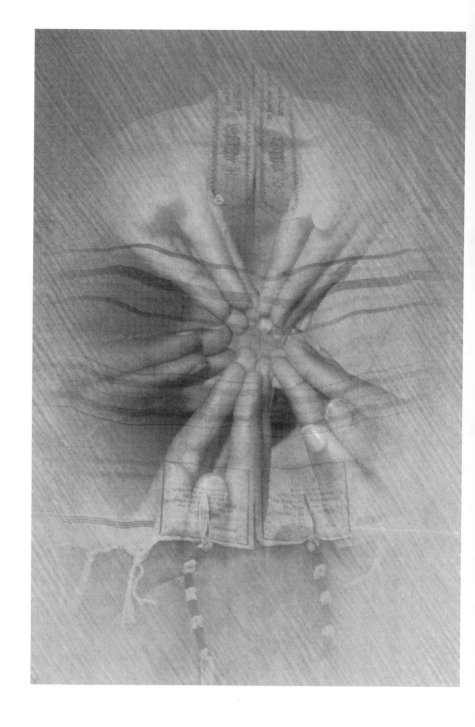

THE FAMILY UNIT - ADULTS

DAY 10 – HUSBANDS

Traditionally our men, our husbands have been the bread winners and providers for the welfare of the families. God has given specific instructions to husbands as to how they are to treat their wives and their children. The husband is the head of the household, the priest and the spiritual leader for his family.

Ephesians 5:25-33 [25]Husbands, love your wives, even as Christ also loved the church, and gave himself for it; [26]That he might sanctify and cleanse it with the washing of water by the word, [27]That he might present it to himself a glorious church, not having spot, or wrinkle, or any such thing; but that it should be holy and without blemish. [28]So ought men to love their wives as their own bodies. He that loveth his wife loveth himself. [29]For no man ever yet hated his own flesh; but nourisheth and cherisheth it, even as the Lord the church: [30]For we are members of his body, of his flesh, and of his bones. [31]For this cause shall a man leave his father and mother, and shall be joined unto his wife, and they two shall be one flesh. [32]This is a great mystery: but I speak concerning Christ and the church. [33]Nevertheless let every one of you in particular so love his wife even as himself; and the wife see that she reverence her husband (KJV).

Prayer

Lord God Almighty, in the name of Jesus, You have set the husband as head of the household and called the wife to be his help mate. Oh Lord, we lift up the husbands to You today and ask You to bless them all. Lead and guide them in paths of righteousness for Your Glory. You knew that the wives would love their husbands, so You called the wives to also honor their husbands. Help them submit to one another and honor each other until they are parted by death. Have mercy on the husbands Lord, and bless them to submit to You and hunger and thirst for Your righteousness. Lord bless the husbands to pray for their wives, their children and their entire households. Bless them to lead their families into prayer and teach the children about the Lord. Give them a clear understanding of Your word and bless them to have bible studies with their families in their homes. Bless them to be those mighty men of valor that You have called them to be in the matchless name of Jesus we pray, Amen.

DAY 11 – FATHERS

When a man becomes a father, his role in the family is expanded. Not only is he responsible for the welfare of his wife, but he is also responsible for his children. God called him to be the head of the family. A part of his responsibility to his children is to teach them about the Lord. Separation or divorce of parents does not change the responsibility of the father to his children. He is still charged with teaching them about God, providing for them and for being present in their lives. Additionally, we can look at the qualifications of the Overseer in 1 Timothy 3:1-7 and see that the attributes of the Overseer also transfer to what a good father and priest of the household should purpose to be and aspire to become.

Ephesians 6:4 ⁴And, ye fathers, provoke not your children to wrath: but bring them up in the nurture and admonition of the Lord (KJV).

1Timothy 3:1-7 ¹This is a true saying, if a man desire the office of a bishop, he desireth a good work. ² A bishop then must be blameless, the husband of one wife, vigilant, sober, of good behaviour, given to hospitality, apt to teach; ³ Not given to wine, no striker, not greedy of filthy lucre; but patient, not a brawler, not covetous; ⁴ One that ruleth well his own house, having his children in subjection with all gravity; ⁵ (For if a man know not how to rule his own house, how shall he take care of the church of God?) ⁶ Not a novice, lest being lifted up with pride he fall into the condemnation of the devil. ⁷ Moreover he must have a good report of them which are without; lest he fall into reproach and the snare of the devil (KJV).

Prayer

Abba our Father, in the name of Jesus, we thank You for knowing each of us so intimately that You know our names. We thank and bless You for caring so much for us that You planned and purposed our lives for Your glory in the beginning. Lord we thank You for blessing us with our earthly fathers. As You watch over us at all times, You have also given us earthly fathers to train us and teach us and show us Your ways. As Joseph taught Jesus and also provided for Jesus, Mary and the Lord's siblings, bless us with fathers who are good role models and providers, men who love the Lord and are mighty men, who seek Your face like never before. We ask You to strengthen our fathers and the men who have provided fatherly guidance in our lives right now. Encourage them Lord when they get discouraged. Bless them with the courage to move forward and to be the priests and heads of their households. Guide their steps in right paths and may Your hand forever be with them. Have Your way in their lives Lord, and use them for Your Glory. Lord draw those fathers who have become separated from their families and bless them to be active participants and present in the lives of all of their children. Bless them to be men of integrity, who are trustworthy, patient and understanding. Lord, we give You praise and thanksgiving for it, in Jesus name we pray, Amen.

DAY 12 – THE POWER OF A PRAYING FATHER

Without fail Job prayed for his children daily, he made sacrifices for them each day. As a father and the priest of your household, it should be your daily practice that you also pray for your children. We are well aware of the things that the enemy has used against us over the years and he will try and use the same things against our children, to steal, kill and destroy. Be wise to pray and cover them each day and ask God to teach them the things that you haven't taught them. Cover them with prayers and the blessing of their Father. Fathers, bless your children. You will find in the Old Testament that the fathers pronounced blessing over their children. To receive a better understanding of the blessings by the fathers, please read the following:

1. Abraham blessing pass on to Isaiah   Genesis 26:1-25

2. Isaiah blessed Jacob and Esau   Genesis 27:26 -40 and Hebrews 11:19-21

3. Jacob blesses his sons   Genesis 49:1-28 and Genesis 48: 1-3

4. Jacob blesses Ephraim and Manasseh and claims them as his own Genesis 48:1- 20 (See also Day 29-Pray Blessing Over Your Children)

Job 1:1-5 1 There was a man in the land of Uz, whose name was Job; and that man was perfect and upright, and one that feared God, and eschewed evil. ² And there were born unto him seven sons and three daughters. ³ His substance also was seven thousand sheep, and three thousand camels, and five hundred yoke of oxen, and five hundred she asses, and a very great household; so that this man was the greatest of all the men of the east. ⁴ And his sons went and feasted in their houses, every one his day; and sent and called for their three sisters to eat and to drink with them. ⁵ And it was so, when the days of their feasting were gone about, that Job sent and sanctified them, and rose up early in the morning, and offered burnt offerings according to the number of them all: for Job said, It may be that my sons have sinned, and cursed God in their hearts. Thus did Job continually (KJV).

Prayer

Lord Jehovah, in the name of Jesus, teach fathers to pray for their children like You prayed for Your disciples. Bless the earthly fathers to seek You until they find You, by seeking You with their whole hearts and all things shall be added unto them. Help them to call upon You for guidance in decision making and teach them how to cover their children, their wives and their households in prayer. Bless them to walk in paths of righteousness and give You glory. Bless them to have a heart for You like David, and encourage them to bless and encourage their own children and families. Give them a heart of flesh where You are the treasure of their hearts. Cause them to chase after You and pass on a legacy to their children of seeking and chasing after the Lord, in Jesus name I pray, Amen.

DAY 13 – ABSENT FATHERS

In the word the man, the father is the head of the household. That is the way that God designed it, however in our society, many today do not want the responsibility of providing for a family nor being faithful to a spouse. A two parent household is still needed, though there are many single parents raising children all along, especially women. The absence of a father is more prevalent than the absence of a mother. There are qualities and traits that both the mother and the father have that are critical to the well upbringing of the children. A mother can raise a son, but there are things that he needs to learn from a man. He needs to know how to treat woman, especially his wife. A daughter needs to hear from her father first how beautiful and wonderful she is, that she is his little princess, how to wait to be found, and learn the qualities and characteristics of a good man. He who finds a wife finds a good thing and receives favor from the Lord (Proverbs 15:22). When there is only one parent in a household there will be an increase in stress and it will be more difficult for that one parent to do the job of both. It's so important that there also be a strong male role model, a brother or uncle in the lives of children where the father is absent. Homosexuality, gay and lesbian lifestyles are becoming more and more common and the absence of a father in the household is leaving a huge vacuum in the family.

Proverbs 27:8 Like a bird that strays from its nest is a man who strays from his home (ESV).

1 Timothy 5:8 But if anyone does not provide for his relatives, and especially for members of his household, he has denied the faith and is worse than an unbeliever (ESV).

Prayer

Abba, Our Father, in the name of Jesus bless Your sons to be the men that You have called them to be. Bless them to be fathers and heads of households leading and guiding their children in the way of the Lord. Let them not fall prey to the pressures of the world and leave their families and children behind to be raised alone. Touch them and anoint them afresh to be men of valor after the heart of the Lord. Strengthen them and bless them, cause them to prosper in the things that they set their hands to do. Guide their every step in the paths that You have designed for them and bring them to an expected end, in Jesus name we pray. All glory, praise and honor to You, our Lord, our Savior and our King, Amen.

DAY 14 – WIVES

When it was time for Adam to have a mate, God did something that He hadn't done with any of His other creations. Out of the ground He had formed all the birds of the air and the animals, even Adam was formed from the dust of the Earth. He made woman as the helper to man, someone who would be comparable to him. So God did the first successful surgery, He took a rib from Adam and used it to form Eve, the first woman and the first wife.

Genesis 2:20-23 [20] So Adam gave names to all cattle, to the birds of the air, and to every beast of the field. But for Adam there was not found a helper comparable to him. [21] And the LORD God caused a deep sleep to fall on Adam, and he slept; and He took one of his ribs, and closed up the flesh in its place. [22] Then the rib which the LORD God had taken from man He made into a woman, and He brought her to the man. [23] And Adam said:

'This *is* now bone of my bones
And flesh of my flesh;
She shall be called Woman,
Because she was taken out of Man (ESV)."

Ephesians 5:22-24, 33 [22]Wives, submit yourselves unto your own husbands, as unto the Lord. [23]For the husband is the head of the wife, even as Christ is the head of the church: and he is the saviour of the body. [24]Therefore as the church is subject unto Christ, so let the wives be to their own husbands in everything. [33]Nevertheless let every one of you in particular so love his wife even as himself; and the wife see that she reverence her husband (KJV).

Prayer

To the only wise God, the God who is, the God who was and the risen Savior and Redeemer who will yet return again, Lord we bless Your name. It is You who made the woman from the rib of Adam and fashioned her in such a manner that a man leaves his father and mother and cleaves to his wife. You have made the wife the help mate for the husband. Lord we ask You today to bless all the wives and keep them in all their ways. Bless them with new vigor and Your prevailing power to overcome all obstacles that stand in their way. Lord bless the wife to honor her husband and to give her husband good advisement. Let her sit at Your feet for Godly counsel and then show her how to advise her husband without attempting to assume his role as the head of the household. Bless her to be a wise woman who always builds her house up and not tear it down in Jesus name we pray, Amen.

DAY 15 – MOTHERS

The Lord made woman as the mate for the husband, and He blessed her to be a wife and then a mother. He made her a nurturer and care giver for her children. Proverbs 31 says that she is a virtuous woman whose price is far more than rubies. She does her husband good all the days of her life and gives to the poor and makes sure that there is good clothing for her family. She keeps her tongue from evil and is not a woman of idleness, she makes good use of her time. She is such an awesome woman that her children and her husband call her blessed and her husband gives her praise.

Genesis 3:20 And Adam called his wife's name Eve; because she was the mother of all living (KJV).

Proverbs 31:10-13,20-21 and 25 – 28 [10]Who can find a virtuous woman? for her price is far above rubies. [11] The heart of her husband doth safely trust in her, so that he shall have no need of spoil. [12] She will do him good and not evil all the days of her life. [13] She seeketh wool, and flax, and worketh willingly with her hands. [20] She stretcheth out her hand to the poor; yea, she reacheth forth her hands to the needy. [21] She is not afraid of the snow for her household: for all her household are clothed with scarlet. [25] Strength and honour are her clothing; and she shall rejoice in time to come. [26] She openeth her mouth with wisdom; and in her tongue is the law of kindness. [27] She looketh well to the ways of her household, and eateth not the bread of idleness. [28] Her children arise up, and call her blessed; her husband also, and he praiseth her (KJV).

Prayer

Heavenly Father, loving Lord, You are a mother to the motherless and a father to the fatherless, in the name of Jesus we give You praise and thanksgiving. It is You who have blessed us with mothers to show us love, who will make great sacrifices just for us and labor before You for our protection and salvation. Thank You for blessing us with mothers who are and were virtuous. You care for us from the cradle to the grave, and You blessed us with an earthly mother who will still call us baby even when our own babies are grown. Lord we thank You! Nobody but You could have made such a one who would change our dirty diapers, wipe our running noses, cook and clean and then count it all joy. We thank You for our mothers and ask You to continue to prosper them, bless them with all spiritual blessing and use them to bring You Glory in Jesus name we pray, Amen.

DAY 16 – THE POWER OF A PRAYING MOTHER

There is much power in prayer and there is something about a mother who prays for her children that I believe that God truly hears. A mother in most cases, no matter what a child has done, still holds onto hope. She will continue to petition the Lord on behalf of her child until there is a turn in the situation. The persistent of the mother in Mark 7:25-30 brought healing to her daughter. Let all mothers continue to press and pray on behalf of their children.

Mark 7:25-30 [25] For a certain woman, whose young daughter had an unclean spirit, heard of him, and came and fell at his feet: [26] The woman was a Greek, a Syrophenician by nation; and she besought him that he would cast forth the devil out of her daughter. [27] But Jesus said unto her, Let the children first be filled: for it is not meet to take the children's bread, and to cast it unto the dogs. [28] And she answered and said unto him, Yes, Lord: yet the dogs under the table eat of the children's crumbs. [29] And he said unto her, For this saying go thy way; the devil is gone out of thy daughter. [30] And when she was come to her house, she found the devil gone out, and her daughter laid upon the bed.

Prayer

Lord You are our Nurturer, at times, You're our Father and Mother, our Comforter. Thank You for being our Role Model and our Chief Intercessor. Thank You for blessing us with an earthly mother who cared and prayed for us. Thank You for raising our mothers up as intercessors and prayer warriors, who labored before You on our behalf. Lord as the mothers petition You daily, hear their cries and bless their children. Cover them, protect them and keep them in all their ways. Bless them to know You and follow You, raise them up as Your own. Lord have your way in the lives of mothers. Move by Your Spirit upon them Lord in Jesus name we pray, Amen.

DAY 17 – THE POWER OF A PRAYING GRANDMOTHER

Timothy was an early minister in the church and he was blessed to be taught by his mother and his grandmother who brought him up in the admonition of the Lord. The influence of both women had a powerful impact on his life. The grandmother trained the mother in the way that she should go and she in turn taught her son Timothy. Timothy was blessed to have both women in his life who both taught him about the Lord. The grandmother's teaching and prayers had an impact on her grandson Timothy, who was her heritage from the Lord. She was blessing the generations who followed her. Timothy's father was a Greek, an unbeliever, and as God would have it, that fact did not hinder Timothy's upbringing in the Lord.

> **2 Timothy 1:5** When I call to remembrance the unfeigned faith that is in thee, which dwelt first in thy grandmother Lois, and thy mother Eunice; and I am persuaded that in thee also (KJV).

> **Acts 16:1-3** Then came he to Derbe and Lystra: and, behold, a certain disciple was there, named Timotheus, the son of a certain woman, which was a Jewess, and believed; but his father was a Greek: ² Which was well reported of by the brethren that were at Lystra and Iconium. ³ Him would Paul have to go forth with him; and took and circumcised him because of the Jews which were in those quarters: for they knew all that his father was a Greek (KJV).

Prayer

Lord God bless us to have a testimony like Lois and Eunice, a praying grandmother and a praying mother. Father bless today's grandmothers to cover and pray for their children's seed and for the generations to come. Abba as Nanna, Nanny, Grand and Grand Mama petition You on behalf of their grandchildren daily, bless their going out and their coming in. Bless them to be the head and not the tail, above only and not beneath. Bless all that they set their hands to do, cause them to prosper, let Your hand always be with them and bless them with Your favor. Bless them to never be wanting, bless their pantries, baskets and barns to always have plenty. Bless them to be givers and bless them to return their riches, talents and resources back to You, their Creator and their Father, in Jesus name, I pray, Amen.

DAY 18 – GRANDPARENTS

So precious to us are our elders, our grandparents, the parents of our parents. Many of them have had to step in and be our champions. They have raised their own children and sometimes find themselves still in the role of parenting, they are raising their children's children. It wasn't by design or the plan, but there are times when the grandparents must step in. There are situations that occur that places them back at the forefront as parents rearing now their grandchildren, ex. an untimely death of their own children, imprisonment, debilitating illness, abandonment, etc. Fortunately this is not the case for all grandparents. As a grandparent, it is a blessing to get to spoil your grandchildren and watch your own children look in amazement and say, "You didn't let me do that." Our children and our grandchildren are our heritage from the Lord. 2 Timothy 1:5 provides a good example of the impact that a grandparent can have in the lives of future generations. Lois the grandmother of Timothy had faith in the Lord which she passed on to her seed for the future generations. Her life set the tone for the spiritual inheritance of her seed.

Proverbs 17:6 ⁶Grandchildren are the crown of the aged, and the glory of children is their fathers (ESV).

2 Timothy 1:5 When I call to remembrance the unfeigned faith that is in thee, which dwelt first in thy grandmother Lois, and thy mother Eunice; and I am persuaded that in thee also (KJV).

Prayer

Adoni, the Lord to whom we all belong, thank You for grandparents who are supportive of their children and their grandchildren. Thank You for their unselfish sacrifices to help, assist and nurture their grandchildren. Bless those who will step in and provide and care for the children when the parents leave and sometimes go astray. Thank You for Your kindness in their lives and for blessing us and our children with the elders who are our grandparents. Thank You Lord for giving them long life and for blessing them to be a blessing to us, in Jesus name, I pray, Amen.

DAY 19 – STEP PARENTS

Some families are blended. A mother or father may separate, divorce and remarry or start a new relationship. This new marriage or relationship may join together 2 households where either one or both partners have children. Immediately having a new parent or a new child can be challenging for all parties in the family, parents and children alike. Everyone will not get along like the Brady Bunch. The job of a step parent is so important and just as it is not easy to be a father or mother, when you are a step parent the task may be even more difficult. Showing favoritism towards one's own children and not being as kind to one's step children can cause additional unnecessary problems. We have got to follow the teaching of the Lord. He is no respecter of persons, He loves us all unconditionally, and what He does for one, He will surely do for another. In families there is often sibling rivalry and we don't want it to be magnified because it can be a root of evil, discord and disunity in the family. A good example in the bible to follow is Joseph, who was the step father of Jesus.

Matthew 1:18-25 [18] Now the birth of Jesus Christ was on this wise: When as his mother Mary was espoused to Joseph, before they came together, she was found with child of the Holy Ghost. [19] Then Joseph her husband, being a just man, and not willing to make her a public example, was minded to put her away privily. [20] But while he thought on these things, behold, the angel of the LORD appeared unto him in a dream, saying, Joseph, thou son of David, fear not to take unto thee Mary thy wife: for that which is conceived in her is of the Holy Ghost. [21] And she shall bring forth a son, and thou shalt call his name JESUS: for he shall save his people from their sins. [22] Now all this was done, that it might be fulfilled which was spoken of the Lord by the prophet, saying, [23] Behold, a virgin shall be with child, and shall bring forth a son, and they shall call his name Emmanuel, which being interpreted is, God with us. [24] Then Joseph being raised from sleep did as the angel of the Lord had bidden him, and took unto him his wife: [25] And knew her not till she had brought forth her firstborn son: and he called his name JESUS (KJV).

Luke Chapter 2 tells you how Joseph took Jesus to the temple to present him to the Lord. He named Him Jesus as the angel of the Lord had told him. He brought him up as his own child. He taught Him his trade as a carpenter. What anguish Joseph and Mary must have felt when Jesus stayed back at the Temple at the age of 12. They didn't know where He was. Verse 51 of Luke 2 says that Jesus went down to Nazareth with Joseph and Mary and was obedient to them. This means to me that Joseph also chastised Him. He brought Him up as a son, not a stepson, but as a son. If you are a stepparent, treat your stepchildren as sons and daughters.

Ephesians 6:1 [1]Children, obey your parents in the Lord, for this is right (NIV).

Romans 12:18 [18]If it is possible, as far as it depends on you, live at peace with everyone (NIV).

Prayer

Emmanuel, the God who is with us, in the name of Jesus, bless us with Your shalom. Bless our homes and cause our families to live together with like minds, like hearts and like spirits, Your Spirit. Lord You said that we should live at peace with everyone. Bless us to live at peace right in our own households. Let us not

show favoritism between children or step children, but bring them all up in the
admonition of the Lord. Bless us to teach them Your word and Your way and to
teach them to be respectful of one another. Let us not take sides or show bias,
bless us to be unified and on one accord and live in harmony within our families.
Lord move us to love and bless that our families be wrapped up, tied up and
tangled up together in You, in Jesus name we pray, Amen.

DAY 20 – FOSTER PARENTS

Esther parents were killed when she was very young and her Uncle Mordecai
took her in and raised her as his own. He was a foster parent and a blood relative.
Pharoah's sister, took Moses in as a babe floating in a basket and claimed him
as her own. She had no blood relationship to him but she raised Moses as a
prince in the palace. Today we have foster parents who are paid by the state to
raise children in their homes. Some do it because they love children and then
there are others who have selfish motives and treat the children harshly. I have
a family member who were raised by foster parents and wherein it was good to
have a roof over his head and not live as an orphan, he indicated that he was
treated cruelly often in his foster home.

> **Exodus 2:1-3,5-10** [1] And there went a man of the house of Levi, and took to
> wife a daughter of Levi. [2] And the woman conceived, and bare a son: and
> when she saw him that he was a goodly child, she hid him three months. [3] And
> when she could not longer hide him, she took for him an ark of bulrushes,
> and daubed it with slime and with pitch, and put the child therein; and she
> laid it in the flags by the river's brink. [5] And the daughter of Pharaoh came
> down to wash herself at the river; and her maidens walked along by the river's
> side; and when she saw the ark among the flags, she sent her maid to fetch
> it. [6] And when she had opened it, she saw the child: and, behold, the babe
> wept. And she had compassion on him, and said, This is one of the Hebrews'
> children. [7] Then said his sister to Pharaoh's daughter, Shall I go and call to
> thee a nurse of the Hebrew women, that she may nurse the child for thee?
> [8] And Pharaoh's daughter said to her, Go. And the maid went and called the

child's mother. [9] And Pharaoh's daughter said unto her, Take this child away, and nurse it for me, and I will give thee thy wages. And the women took the child, and nursed it. [10] And the child grew, and she brought him unto Pharaoh's daughter, and he became her son. And she called his name Moses: and she said, Because I drew him out of the water (KJV).

Esther 2:7 And he brought up Hadassah, that is, Esther, his uncle's daughter: for she had neither father nor mother, and the maid was fair and beautiful; whom Mordecai, when her father and mother were dead, took for his own daughter (KJV).

Prayer

To Elohim, our Creator, the God who never leaves us nor forsakes us, the One who is our Mother and Father, in Jesus name, thank You Lord for foster parents. Use them in the lives of Your children Lord to raise them in the way of the Lord. Bless the orphaned children to be placed in homes where they are loved and cared for and wanted. Bless them not to be abused, but nurtured like Mordecai nurtured and blessed Esther. Keep watch over them day and night Lord. Encourage them, strengthen them and never leave them alone. Protect them from those who desire to do them harm and have Your way in their lives, let Your will be done, in Jesus name I pray, Amen.

PRAYER TARGETS AND PERSONAL NOTES

_____

_____

_____

_____

_____

_____

_____

_____

_____

_____

_____

_____

_____

_____

_____

_____

_____

_____

_____

_____

_____

_____

_____

_____

_____
_____
_____
_____
_____
_____
_____
_____
_____
_____
_____
_____
_____
_____
_____
_____
_____
_____
_____
_____
_____
_____
_____
_____
_____
_____
_____
_____

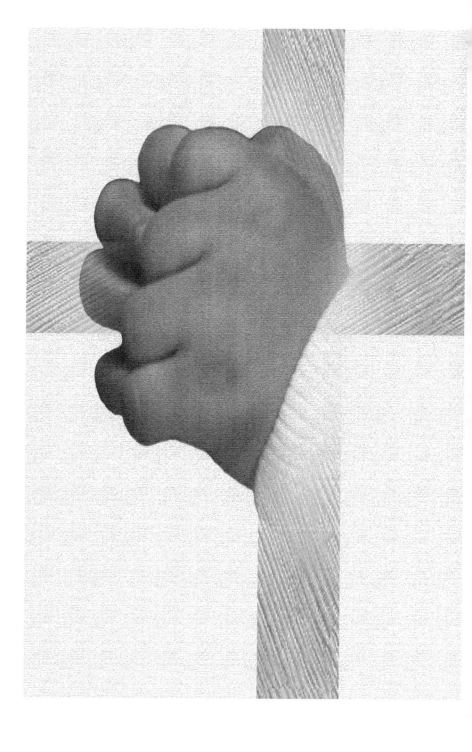

TARGETED PRAYER FOR OUR CHILDREN

DAY 21 – CHILDREN

Our children are truly our heritage and a blessing from the Lord. It is our children and our children's children who continue to carry the legacy of our families. Lord as you first loved us, You placed such anticipation in our heart for our unborn children, we get some idea of what it must be like to love unconditionally. Once they arrive, You bless us to lead and guide them in the ways of the Lord. For those who follow You, our offspring and seed are blessed for a thousand generations to come, Halleluiah! You don't forsake the righteous and the seed of the righteous do not beg for bread. You ably provide for us and our offspring. You are Jehovah Jireh our provider and are constantly taking care of our every need. Thank You Lord, for blessing us with our seed and for providing us with our daily bread.

Ephesians 6:1-3 [1]Children, obey your parents in the Lord: for this is right. [2]Honour thy father and mother; which is the first commandment with promise; [3]That it may be well with thee, and thou mayest live long on the earth (KJV).

Prayer

El Shaddai, Lord God Almighty, You're awesome, majestic and perfect in all Your ways. In Jesus name Lord, I thank You for the blessing of my offspring and seed who are my children, for every good and perfect gift comes from above. At an early age Lord, our children's minds are so impressionable, Lord bless them to be led by Your Spirit. Help them to stand and not fold when pressed by their peers to stray from Your teachings and divert the plans that You have for them. Bless their teachers to be knowledgeable, effective and sensitive to Your Spirit. Bless their schools to be places of wisdom and honesty and keep them safe there from all harm. Bless them Lord with gifts and talents from on high, stir up their gifts and increase Your power in the gifts that You have given them. Smear them with Your anointing to give You glory. Help them walk through all the doors that You have open and available to them for Your Glory Lord, in Jesus name I pray. Lord I give You praise and thanksgiving for my children, Amen.

DAY 21 – CONTINUED STEP CHILDREN

When you look for a definition of step children, you will find many dictionaries will say they are the children of a spouse from a previous union. In addition, you may see this description, something or someone who does not receive respect, proper attention or appropriate care. Unfortunately there are many people who will not appreciate their step children, however I thank God for those who will treat them with dignity and respect and raise them as their own. In fact, they will not refer to them as their step children, but rather as their own children. Where it not for step children, some of us would not have had the opportunity to receive that special love that only comes from a parent and child relationship, which is a bond like none other. Our scripture tells the story of how Hosea, a prophet marries Gomer, who bears him a son and then has 2 other children. As you research the scriptures the other 2 children are not Hosea's, for his wife, Gomer is involved in adulterous relationships. In Chapter 2, she leaves him and goes out and has other lovers, then in Chapter 3, he takes her back. Hosea takes her back and now has 3 children, 2 of whom he did not father. He takes them into his home as his own. Every child is important to God. You may not be asked by God to marry someone who is going to be unfaithful to you, but you may be needed by God to raise a child who may otherwise be motherless, fatherless or unloved. Remember the golden rule? **Matthew 7:12** Therefore all things whatsoever ye would that men should do to you, do ye even so to them: for this is the law and the prophets (KJV). There but for the grace of God this could have been you; you could have been the one who was motherless or fatherless.

Hosea 1:2-6 ......And the LORD said to Hosea, Go, take unto thee a wife of whoredoms and children of whoredoms: for the land hath committed great whoredom, departing from the LORD. ³ So he went and took Gomer the daughter of Diblaim; which conceived, and bare him a son. ⁴ And the LORD said unto him, Call his name Jezreel; for yet a little while, and I will avenge the blood of Jezreel upon the house of Jehu, and will cause to cease the kingdom of the house of Israel. ⁵ And it shall come to pass at that day, that I will break the bow of Israel, in the valley of Jezreel. ⁶ And she conceived again, and bare a daughter. And God said unto him, Call her name Loruhamah: for I will no more have mercy upon the house of Israel; but I will utterly take them away. ⁷ But I will have mercy upon the house of Judah, and will save them by the LORD their God, and will not save them by bow, nor by sword, nor by battle, by horses, nor by horsemen. ⁸ Now when she had weaned Loruhamah, she conceived, and bare a son (KJV).

Hosea 3:1-3 The LORD said to me, "Go, show your love to your wife again, though she is loved by another man and is an adulteress. Love her as the LORD loves the Israelites, though they turn to other gods and love the sacred raisin cakes." ² So I bought her for fifteen shekels[a] of silver and about a homer and a lethek[b] of barley. ³ Then I told her, "You are to live with me many days; you must not be a prostitute or be intimate with any man, and I will behave the same way toward you (NIV)."

Prayer

Heavenly Father, Lover of my soul, in the name of Jesus, I come before You today to give You honor, glory and praise. You are a kind and loving God, slow to anger and abounding in love. Bless Your name, sweet Jesus, bless Your holy name. Lord You are the One who has blessed many children to have parents and step parents who love them and care for them. I plead the blood of Jesus over the children who will be mistreated by step parents and will feel unloved and leave home. Have mercy upon the step children who will be rebellious because they didn't want a new father or mother in their lives. Lord cause all the step parents and the step children to love one another and make sacrifices to keep the peace and spread the love within their families. Help them to treat each other as they desire to be treated. Bless that there be no competition between the children and the parents for the love of the other parent. Merciful Father, bless that there be reconciliation in marriages where there has been separation because of problems between step parents and step children. May there be peace, love, joy, harmony and unity in all these households, in Jesus name, I pray, Amen.

DAY 22 – SIBLINGS – BROTHERS AND SISTERS

Andrew brought his brother Cephas, whom Jesus later named Peter to follow Christ and Peter became one of the major apostles of Christ. David had several wives and several sets of different children and envy and lust lead to one of them (Amnon) raping his sister Tamar (2 Samuel 13:1-14). Tamar's brother Absolon, 2 years later came back and killed Amnon (2 Samuel 13:23-29). Later this same son Absalom sought to kill his father David. Joseph the dreamer had 10 of his 11 brothers who hated him, but Joseph later saved the entire family of Jacob/Israel when he brought them to Egypt during a great famine (Genesis Chapters 47 and 48). Our brothers and sisters really are our keepers and we should treat them accordingly.

> **John 1:40-42** [40] One of the two which heard John speak, and followed him, was Andrew, Simon Peter's brother. [41] He first findeth his own brother Simon, and saith unto him, We have found the Messias, which is, being interpreted,

the Christ. [42] And he brought him to Jesus. And when Jesus beheld him, he said, Thou art Simon the son of Jona: thou shalt be called Cephas, which is by interpretation, A stone (KJV).

Prayer

Father God, I thank You for my siblings, and I thank You for keeping us all. We have grown up side-by-side and know many intimate details about one another that we shall never share with another person, other than You. Bless us to be like Andrew and share our love for You with our siblings. Lord bless us even when we disagree to always show love towards each other. Bless us not to have competitive spirits, but be compassionate, kind and considerate. Save our siblings Lord from every trick and every snare of the enemy, bless that their souls be saved by You and bless them to walk with You beside the still waters in Jesus name. With a humble heart I ask You to cleanse them and heal them, make them anew again, in Jesus Name, I pray, Amen.

DAY 23   SIBLING RIVALRY

Cain and Abel is the first story of sibling rivalry in the word, unfortunately it's not the last. As stated in Ecclesiastes; there is nothing new under the sun, and you will see sibling rivalry and it's ugly head rise again in scripture. Competition is good for sports, however a competitive spirit can be very destructive, especially within the family. You will find there were many other cases of sibling rivalry recorded within the word. You may want to read about Esau and Jacob (Genesis Chapter 27) and Joseph and his brothers (Genesis Chapter 37). In addition read about the sons of David in 2 Samuel, Chapter 13. Admiration of a sibling's accomplishments may cause another sibling to strive to do better and be encouraged that if my brother or sister excelled, so can I. In a healthy family environment siblings counsel one another to not travel the paths that lead to wickedness, but instead to righteousness. They don't want their brothers and sisters to make the same mistakes they have made. I admire how Andrew brought his brother Peter to the Lord. He didn't keep a good thing to himself, he shared, for yes we are our brother's keeper.

Genesis 4:1-10 [1]And Adam knew Eve his wife; and she conceived, and bare Cain, and said, I have gotten a man from the LORD. [2]And she again bare his brother Abel. And Abel was a keeper of sheep, but Cain was a tiller of the ground. [3]And in process of time it came to pass, that Cain brought of the fruit of the ground an offering unto the LORD. [4]And Abel, he also brought of the firstlings of his flock and of the fat thereof. And the LORD had respect unto Abel and to his offering: [5]But unto Cain and to his offering he had not respect. And Cain was very wroth, and his countenance fell. [6]And the LORD said unto Cain, Why art thou wroth? and why is thy countenance fallen? [7]If thou doest well, shalt thou not be accepted? and if thou doest not well, sin lieth at the door. And unto thee shall be his desire, and thou shalt rule over him. [8]And Cain talked with Abel his brother: and it came to pass, when they were in the field, that Cain rose up against Abel his brother, and slew him. [9]And the LORD said unto Cain, Where is Abel thy brother? And he said, I know not: Am I my brother's keeper? [10]And he said, What hast thou done? the voice of thy brother's blood crieth unto me from the ground.

Prayer

Holy God, awesome God, mighty in all Your ways, in the name of Jesus, I give You praise. I thank You Lord for another day, and I bless You for my brothers and sisters and their families. Forgive us Lord for allowing rivalries to separate and pull us apart. Forgive us for being competitive and looking for opportunities to tear down instead of building up. Forgive all our sins Lord and bless us once again to live at peace with our brothers and our sisters, in Jesus name. Bless us Lord not to compete with one another, instead bless us to encourage one another to greatness. Let us agree that we can disagree on a matter and still move forward in love in Jesus name. Bless us to offer a helping hand and bridle our tongues. Let us not speak evil of one another, instead let us speak blessings over the lives of our sisters and our brothers, in Jesus name, I pray. Holy God, Awesome God, Mighty

God, I give You praise and thanksgiving, for You are a restorer. Restore our relationships with one another and bless us to walk in agreement, side-by-side, in Jesus name I pray. I bless You and thank You for it Lord, Amen.

DAY 24 – DISCIPLINING OUR CHILDREN – LAYING ON OF HANDS

As the Lord loves us and chastises us, so we should love our children and chastise them. There is still a need for disciplining children. For so many families parenting today, spanking is a thing of the past. Placing children in time out, is the modern way. For many children, time out is not going to work. Spanking at an early age will work with most children to teach them discipline. As they get older removing or disallowing things that they really like will get their attention (video games, phones, social networking, even cut or remove their allowance for a period of time). It's more important to have the respect of your children than to concern yourself with being their BFF (best friend forever). They may even hate you for a time, but they will get over it. More than anything, talk with them at an early age about all subjects, don't take anything off the table. Be willing to be transparent about your own life. Let them hear your views on the subject matter. The world and their friends will surely tell them theirs. Do more than just say don't do this, give them the why nots and please don't offer a poor example with your own life, no do as I say and not as I do. They will immolate what they see you do. Be a good role model, they are watching you.

Proverbs 13:24 ²⁴He that spareth his rod hateth his son: but he that loveth him chasteneth him betimes (KJV).

Deuteronomy 8:5 ⁵Thou shalt also consider in thine heart, that, as a man chasteneth his son, so the LORD thy God chasteneth thee (KJV).

Hebrews 12:6-7 ⁶For whom the Lord loveth he chasteneth, and scourgeth every son whom he receiveth. ⁷If ye endure chastening, God dealeth with you as with sons; for what son is he whom the father chasteneth not (KJV).

Prayer

Our Father, in the name of Your Son Jesus, hallowed be Your blessed and holy name. Lord You discipline us because You love us, bless us to discipline our children because we love them. Help us to not be so concerned about being their friends, but be their parents and admonish them in the ways of the Lord. Bless us to warn them about evil and also give them praise for the good things they do. Teach us how to discipline our children at every age and lead them into paths of righteous that lead directly to You. Order their steps in right paths. Be a lamp unto their feet and a light unto their paths. Lord help us to show mercy but also that tough love that is needed so they won't go astray. Lord God, cause our children to lie down in verdant pastures, lead them beside the still and calm waters and restore their souls. Bless Lord that Your kingdom come and Your will be done in the lives of our children in Jesus name, I pray, Amen.

DAY 25 – TEACHING OUR CHILDREN TO PRAY, PRAYING WITH THEM

The word says whoever shall receive the Kingdom of God like a small child shall be the one to enter into God's Kingdom. Adults can surely learn a lot from the character of little children. Children trust easily especially their parents. They will jump off of a counter into the arms of their parents trusting all the way that their parents will catch them and take care of them. Doubt doesn't enter their minds, they just dash forth. Out of the mouths of babes questions come forth that others may be afraid to ask. The little children just want to know the reason why. They don't use big words or pretenses, just simply keeping it real. They may not want to share their toys and will sometimes fight, but they also forgive and forget quickly and are friends again in an instance. Our own battles may be much greater, but we can do all things through Christ who strengthens us and remember also that there is nothing too hard for God.

So teach them to pray as like having a conversation with God. Thank you God for my Mommy and Daddy, bless them God. I didn't like Tommy taking my toy today, but I am glad that he is my friend. Forgive me for being a bad boy or girl (whatever is applicable) today. I promise to do better, Amen. One last thing, as they continue to grow older, pray with them as a family, always leave the door open for them to be transparent with you. Listen, don't judge, ask God to keep them and cover them and teach you how to be there for them through the storms and victories of life. Remember, you where a kid once and you were also, immature.

A Child's Prayer

Lord, I am just a child, but I know You are there. Teach me how to pray and what to say. I love my mom and my dad and my sisters and my brothers. Lord bless them and bless all the little children like me. Teach us all how to pray so we can be with You and Jesus someday, Amen.

> **Mark 10:13-16** [13] And they brought young children to him, that he should touch them: and his disciples rebuked those that brought them. [14] But when Jesus saw it, he was much displeased, and said unto them, Suffer the little children to come unto me, and forbid them not: for of such is the kingdom of God. [15] Verily I say unto you, Whosoever shall not receive the kingdom of God as a little child, he shall not enter therein. [16] And he took them up in his arms, put his hands upon them, and blessed them (KJV).

Prayer

El Shaddai, Lord God Almighty, in the name of Jesus, You said that Your house is a house of prayer. As You have taught me to pray, help me to teach my children to pray. Bless us to pray together as a family and to petition You daily even when we are apart. You are Abba, my Father and their Father and Your name is greater than any name. Let Your kingdom continue to come Lord in every way, keep me and my children so that none be lost Lord. When they are afraid, remind them of Your perfect love which cast out all fear. When I am troubled and they see me concerned, bless us to come together and pray and give the matter to You Lord who care for me and my children. I come against everything that would hinder our prays and keep us from seeking You Lord. I command mountains to move out of my way and our way and I cast them into the sea, in Jesus name I pray, Amen. To God be the glory for all that He has done.

DAY 26 – NURTURING THE GIFTS AND TALENTS OF YOUR CHILDREN

Each child will have their own separate and distinct personality, even as a baby of just a few days old has his own way of expressing his needs. As they grow you will quickly learn their likes and dislikes, observe and learn their strengths and weaknesses. Be attentive to knowing their gifts and talents. When you see your children excelling in a specific area, build them up and speak encouraging words. Ask the Lord to stir up their gifts and use them for His Glory. When possible help them to develop that gift or talent. It may very well be a part of the calling that God has on their life. The games they enjoy playing may even give some insight to the things that God has purposed for their life. A finger painter today may be a Van Gogh tomorrow.

Colossians 3:23-24 [23] Whatever you do, work at it with all your heart, as working for the Lord, not for human masters, [24] since you know that you will receive an inheritance from the Lord as a reward. It is the Lord Christ you are serving (NIV).

1 Corinthians 14:12 [12] So it is with you. Since you are eager for gifts of the Spirit, try to excel in those that build up the church (NIV).

Romans 12:6-8 [6] We have different gifts, according to the grace given to each of us. If your gift is prophesying, then prophesy in accordance with your[a] faith; [7] if it is serving, then serve; if it is teaching, then teach; [8] if it is to encourage, then give encouragement; if it is giving, then give generously; if it is to lead,[b] do it diligently; if it is to show mercy, do it cheerfully (NIV).

James 1:17 [17] Every good and perfect gift is from above, coming down from the Father of the heavenly lights, who does not change like shifting shadows (NIV).

Romans 12:11 [11] Never be lacking in zeal, but keep your spiritual fervor, serving the Lord (NIV).

Prayer

Lord, in the name of Jesus, You are my Everything. You're my Master, my Waymaker the Giver of good gifts and You are my Gift of Life. Thank You for caring and nurturing me and blessing me to be a nurturer of my children. As I watch over them and train them in Your ways, help me to see the gifts that You have placed within each of them. Help me to encourage them to excel and practice and use the gifts and talents that You have blessed them with within their minds, bodies, souls and spirits. Bless and make prosperous the things that they set their hands to do within Your kingdom. Give them favor in every area of their lives to encourage, to lead, to give, to show mercy and to do it cheerfully. Bless them to have a zest for You and to be enthusiastic and work with passion and fervor in Your kingdom, in Jesus name, I pray, Amen.

DAY 27 – TEACH YOUR CHILDREN TO GIVE

Children watch and observe, they learn by what they see you do, so show them good examples of giving and sharing. Lead by example. Don't just let them place your envelope in the offering basket, be sure to give them money for their own envelope. Tell them what a tithe and an offering is and why they should give. Volunteer at a shelter and take them with you. Donate clothes, shovel a neighbor's driveway, cut the widows grass, visit the elderly and read to them. Let them see that giving goes well beyond money, but also giving of oneself and of your time is so very valuable.

Proverbs 11:25 ²⁵ The liberal soul shall be made fat: and he that watereth shall be watered also himself (KJV).

Luke 6:38 ³⁸ Give, and it shall be given unto you; good measure, pressed down, and shaken together, and running over, shall men give into your bosom. For with the same measure that ye mete withal it shall be measured to you again (KJV).

Prayer

Jehovah Jirah, my Provider, the One who gave His one and only begotten Son so that I might be free, Lord I bless Your name. Bless me to be a cheerful giver and teach my offspring and seed to follow Your example of giving. Bless us to lend a helping hand to those in need and help someone else move from poverty to comfort. Let us not just give from our lips but also from our hearts and hands. Lord God, You are our Source, bless me and my children for generations to come to be givers and bless the kingdom of God, in Jesus name I pray, Amen.

DAY 28 – LEAVING AN INHERITANCE FOR YOUR CHILDREN

The bible says in <u>Proverbs 13:22</u> A good man leaveth an **inheritance** to his children's children: and the wealth of the sinner is laid up for the just. Yes, it is a good thing to leave your children with finances, resources, trust funds and homes, but don't forget to teach them about God, how to pray and how to handle money. Our primary objective should be to leave our heritage (our children) a foundation of trusting, believing and depending upon God. We should teach them to pray continually as stated in **I Thessalonians 5:17** Pray without ceasing (KJV); and to **Philippians 4:6** Be careful for nothing; but in everything by prayer and supplication with thanksgiving let your requests be made known unto God (KJV).

As a parent (grandparent), guardian or care taker when you pray, ask God to forgive you for the things that you have not taught your children and ask Him to teach them His ways and His word. Lastly, then trust Him as He answers these requests. In the natural it may not always look good, because they too will go through trials and tribulation. However, He is the God who works everything together for the good of those who love Him and who are called according to His purpose (Romans 8:28).

When we seek Him first for all things, everything that we need is added unto us (Matthew 6:33). It pleases Him that we seek Him first, for He is a wonderful counselor. He knows the past, the present and the future. He also knows the plans that He has for you and for your children, and that is to prosper and grow not to harm you or them, but to give you both hope and a future, to bring all of you and yours to an expected end (Jeremiah 29:11). When you please Him, he will reward you. Solomon wrote in Ecclesiastes 2: 26 To the man who pleases Him, God gives wisdom, knowledge and happiness, but to the sinner He gives the task of gathering and storing up wealth to hand it over to the one who pleases God.......(NIV).

Some believe in I got mine, you get yours. Most unfortunately, they have that same attitude towards their own, their children. Yes we need our children to learn, but we should also train them up in the way that they should go and when they get old, they shall not part from it (Proverbs 22:6). Teach them more than just how to make money, teach them to use it to bless others for God. Teach them this at a young age. This training shall not be in vain. It's a down payment on prosperity for your children's children for generations to come. It is God who gives us the ability to acquire wealth (Deuteronomy 8:18) and all good and perfect gifts come from above (James 1:17).

I was traveling on my way home some years ago and I asked an elderly woman on the airplane what advice would she share with others about finances. Consider her a wise woman for she said, "There is no honest work beneath you." Here's a perfect example. When my children were very young, God blessed me to be a homemaker. There were years where I had very little or no personal income. While it was a sacrifice, I knew it was a blessing. I considered staying home with them as this; it's better to pay on the front end, than the back end. Time invested in them when they were young would pay off on the good citizens they would grow up and become. Train up a child in the way that he should go and when he gets old, he shall not part.

While you are training and teaching them, teach them how to save for emergencies and the future, not to hoard, but to share. Teach them about giving, tithing and giving their offerings, and to give of their time and talents. Life skills are important for not just their generation, but the next and the next. Don't let the world teach them about credit without their having a biblical prospective. The word says we are not borrowers but lenders. So teach them how to be a lender, teach them to give.

Psalm 115:13-14 [13] He will bless them that fear the LORD, both small and great. [14] The LORD shall increase you more and more, you and your children (KJV).

Psalm 127:3-5 [3] Lo, children are an heritage of the LORD: and the fruit of the womb is his reward. [4] As arrows are in the hand of a mighty man; so are children of the youth. [5] Happy is the man that hath his quiver full of them: they shall not be ashamed, but they shall speak with the enemies in the gate (KJV).

Proverbs 19:17 [17] He that hath pity upon the poor lendeth unto the LORD; and that which he hath given will he pay him again (KJV).

Proverbs 28:27 [27] He that giveth unto the poor shall not lack: but he that hideth his eyes shall have many a curse (KJV).

Isaiah 54:13 [13] And all thy children shall be taught of the LORD; and great shall be the peace of thy children (KJV).

Isaiah 60:4 [4] Lift up thine eyes round about, and see: all they gather themselves together, they come to thee: thy sons shall come from far, and thy daughters shall be nursed at thy side (KJV).

Prayer

My Heavenly Father in the name of Jesus You have blessed me with my children, my heritage, my seed. I thank You for loaning them to me during this their earthly existence. I bless You now for the joy they have brought into my life. Truly You are the Giver of good gifts and I thank You for the great gift of my children. Lord an inheritance in You is what I desire to leave with my children. An inheritance in praying and seeking Your face and trusting and believing in You is the greatest inheritance that I can leave them. Father grant that it happen in Jesus name I pray. I'm purposing my life to be obedient and faithful to You. And I thank You now for my children know of You and thank You for saving my children for generations to come. Lord let Your glory fall upon my children and bless them with spiritual gifts and stir up their gifts in the name of Jesus. Increase Your power more and more in their gifts and let them serve You in humility and seek Your face daily. When their enemies seek to overtake them, Lord I know that You will never leave them nor forsake them. Lord, Jehovah rebuke the devourer and break the oppressor into pieces, contend with the one who contends with my children, In Jesus name, I pray.

Lord I thank You and I give You praise for Your peace that fills my children; Lord grant them peace in all that they set their hands to do in Jesus name. Father God as they be in health cause their souls to prosper in Jesus name. Lord as You lead and guide them into all truths, teach them about giving of their time, talents and resources. God I thank You now for my children marrying the spouses that You have chosen for them. Lord I program these prayers into the heavens and I pray that they continually be a sweet fragrance in Your nostrils throughout generations to come in Jesus name, Amen.

DAY 29 – PRAY BLESSINGS OVER YOUR CHILDREN

It was the practice of the Israelites to past on a blessing to their children. Abraham blessed Isaiah, Isaiah blessed Jacob and Esau and we see listed below the blessing of Jacob for his 12 sons, the 12 tribes of Israel. We are in position to bless our children by training them up in the way that they should go. They should know of the Lord and be taught about His way and His word. We don't just bless them with a financial inheritance, but with an inheritance in the Lord. Speak words of life and encouragement over your children daily. Always intercede for them through daily prayer. Pray and speak blessing over them constantly, it's your responsibility (see Day 12 – The Power of a Praying Father for more scripture on fathers blessing their children). Speak life not death, the power of life and death is in the tongue (Proverbs 18:21).

Genesis 49:1-28 [1] And Jacob called unto his sons, and said, Gather yourselves together, that I may tell you that which shall befall you in the last days. [2] Gather yourselves together, and hear, ye sons of Jacob; and hearken unto Israel your father. [3] Reuben, thou art my firstborn, my might, and the beginning of my strength, the excellency of dignity, and the excellency of power: [4] Unstable as water, thou shalt not excel; because thou wentest up to thy father's bed; then defiledst thou it: he went up to my couch. [5] Simeon and Levi are brethren; instruments of cruelty are in their habitations. [6] O my soul, come not thou into their secret; unto their assembly, mine honour, be not thou united: for in their anger they slew a man, and in their selfwill they digged down a wall. [7] Cursed be their anger, for it was fierce; and their wrath, for it was cruel: I will divide them in Jacob, and scatter them in Israel. [8] Judah, thou art he whom thy brethren shall praise: thy hand shall be in the neck of thine enemies; thy father's children shall bow down before thee. [9] Judah is a lion's whelp: from the prey, my son, thou art gone up: he stooped down, he couched as a lion, and as an old lion; who shall rouse him up? [10] The sceptre shall not depart from Judah, nor a lawgiver from between his feet, until Shiloh come; and unto him shall the gathering of the people be. [11] Binding his foal unto the vine, and his ass's colt unto the choice vine; he washed his garments in wine, and his clothes in the blood of grapes: [12] His eyes shall be red with wine, and his teeth white with milk. [13] Zebulun shall dwell at the haven of the sea; and he shall be for an haven of ships; and his border shall be unto Zidon. [14] Issachar is a strong ass couching down between two burdens: [15] And he saw that rest was good, and the land that it was pleasant; and bowed his shoulder to bear, and became a servant unto tribute. [16] Dan shall judge his people, as one of the tribes of Israel. [17] Dan shall be a serpent by the way, an adder in the path, that biteth the horse heels, so that his rider shall fall backward. [18] I have waited for thy salvation, O LORD. [19] Gad, a troop shall overcome him: but he shall overcome at the last. [20] Out of Asher his bread shall be fat, and he shall yield royal dainties. [21] Naphtali is a hind let loose: he giveth goodly words. [22] Joseph is a fruitful bough, even a fruitful bough by a well; whose branches run over the wall: [23] The archers have sorely grieved him, and shot at him, and hated him: [24] But his bow abode in strength, and the arms of his hands were made strong by the hands of the mighty God of Jacob; (from thence is the shepherd, the stone of Israel:) ²⁵ Even by the God of thy father, who shall help thee; and by the Almighty, who shall bless thee with blessings of heaven above, blessings of the deep that lieth under, blessings of the breasts, and of the womb: ²⁶ The blessings of thy father have prevailed above the blessings of my progenitors unto the utmost bound of the everlasting hills: they shall be on the head of Joseph, and on the crown of the head of him that was separate from his brethren. ²⁷ Benjamin shall ravin as a wolf: in the morning he shall devour the prey, and at night he shall divide the spoil. ²⁸ All these are the twelve tribes of Israel: and this is it that their father spake unto them, and blessed them; every one according to his blessing he blessed them (KJV).

Prayer

Elohim our Creator, in the name of Jesus, we bless Your name. From the rising of the sun until the going down of the same, You Lord are worthy of our praise. Father we bless our children for generations to come and ask You to bless them with all spiritual blessings. Father bless their going out and their coming in. Watch over them and encamp Your angels around them to keep them in all their ways. Lord add special blessings to our children mentally, spiritually, emotionally, physically and financially in Jesus name we pray. We decree and declare that our children are the head and not the tail. They are above only and not beneath. They have victory in their lives and are conquerors through Christ Jesus. They are blessed in the city and in the land. They are lenders and not borrowers. They are blessed and have the favor of their Father. We thank You Lord for the abundant blessings flowing upon our children, in Jesus name, we pray, Amen.

DAY 30 – RUN-A-WAYS

The prodigal son we're going to use today as a story of a run-a-way. He was one who ran off with his inheritance at an early age. He did not wait for his father to die and leave him an inheritance, but asked his father for it while his father was yet alive, and his father obliged him. He quickly went through all that he had by being wasteful, extravagant and reckless. He spent it all.

Luke 15:11-24 [11] And he said, A certain man had two sons: [12] And the younger of them said to his father, Father, give me the portion of goods that falleth to me. And he divided unto them his living. [13] And not many days after the younger son gathered all together, and took his journey into a far country, and there wasted his substance with riotous living. [14] And when he had spent all, there arose a mighty famine in that land; and he began to be in want. [15] And he went and joined himself to a citizen of that country; and he sent him into his fields to feed swine. [16] And he would fain have filled his belly with the husks that the swine did eat: and no man gave unto him. [17] And when he came to himself, he said, How many hired servants of my father's have bread enough and to spare, and I perish with hunger! [18] I will arise and go to my father, and will say unto him, Father, I have sinned against heaven, and before thee, [19] And am no more worthy to be called thy son: make me as one of thy hired servants. [20] And he arose, and came to his father. But when he was yet a great way off, his father saw him, and had compassion, and ran, and fell on his neck, and kissed him. [21] And the son said unto him, Father, I have sinned against heaven, and in thy sight, and am no more worthy to be called thy son. [22] But the father said to his servants, Bring forth the best robe, and put it on him; and put a ring on his hand, and shoes on his feet: [23] And bring hither the fatted calf, and kill it; and let us eat, and be merry: [24] For this my son was dead, and is alive again; he was lost, and is found. And they began to be merry.

Prayer

Most gracious and precious Lord, Creator of heaven and earth, Keeper of my soul, in the name of Jesus I give You praise and thanksgiving for all my children for generations to come. Today Lord, I thank You for keeping them from danger, traps, sickness and snares. Lord I pray that Your mighty hand always be with them and that You keep them from all hurt and harm so that they do not grieve and do not cause pain. Lord bless these Your children who have run away from You spiritually and their families physically. Lord help them find their way back to Your arms back home where they belong. Let them rush into Your warm embrace and be comforted right now in the name of Jesus, like never before.

Bless them also Lord to return home to their earthly mothers and fathers in Jesus name, I pray. Father I bind up all disunity in the family, all anger and fear and cast it to dry places. I command the spirit of rebellion to dry up and go from our children right now in the name of Jesus. As the prodigal son came to his senses and returned home from a foreign land, Lord return all run-a-way children to their parents and guardians in Jesus name. Thank You sweet Jesus, for caring for them, protecting them and watching over them, Amen.

DAY 31 – MISSING CHILDREN

What anguish a parent must feel to have a child that is missing. Only God can take a situation like that and use it for His glory. In Genesis, there is an account of how Joseph was favored by his father Jacob and was given a coat of many colors. He dreams that he is more esteemed than his brothers. They become angry and jealous, desire to kill him, but later sell him into slavery. He ends up in Egypt first in Pontiphar's house, whose wife accuses him of molesting her because he would not sleep with her. Next he goes to prison and God shows him great favor everywhere he goes. Eventually he ends up second in charge of all Egypt. There is a big famine in all the lands and Egypt because they followed the plans of Joseph are the only ones with food. It's an exciting story, you've got to read the entire account in Genesis chapters 37-47. Ultimately, he saved Jacob and his entire household and the son whom Jacob was afraid was dead is yet alive.

If we go to the New Testament we will find an account of how our Lord and Savior, Jesus Christ as a child stayed back at the temple after one of the holy feast and his parents, Mary and Joseph, did not know where he was. Read the account below.

Luke 2:42-50 [42] And when he was twelve years old, they went up to Jerusalem after the custom of the feast. [43] And when they had fulfilled the days, as they returned, the child Jesus tarried behind in Jerusalem; and Joseph and his mother knew not of it. [44] But they, supposing him to have been in the company, went a day's journey; and they sought him among their kinsfolk and acquaintance. ⁴⁵ And when they found him not, they turned back again to Jerusalem, seeking him. ⁴⁶ And it came to pass, that after three days they found him in the temple, sitting in the midst of the doctors, both hearing them, and asking them questions. ⁴⁷ And all that heard him were astonished at his understanding and answers. ⁴⁸ And when they saw him, they were amazed: and his mother said unto him, Son, why hast thou thus dealt with us? behold, thy father and I have sought thee sorrowing. ⁴⁹ And he said unto them, How is it that ye sought me? wist ye not that I must be about my Father's business? ⁵⁰ And they understood not the saying which he spake unto them (KJV).

We know that there are many situations in which children go missing and are never found again. Let's pray today that God will reveal the locations of all missing children alive and dead and pray for justice for them, Amen.

Prayer

Father God in the name of Jesus, You see and know all things. You have eyes that see, ears that hear, hands that hold and comfort and a mouth that speaks. Lord You are great and mighty and greatly to be praised. There is no one greater than you Lord! You know the locations of all missing children, the run-a-ways, the ones who have been taken by other family members, even the ones who have been kidnaped and abducted. Lord expose their where-a-bouts, protect them and keep them safe from all harm. Comfort their parents and families Lord, and bless them with Your peace in the midst of the storm. Lord You said that Your eyes are upon the righteous and Your ears are attentive to their cries. Lord hear our petitions today, be with all the missing children right now Lord. Place a strong hedge of protection around them, calm them from their fears. Let Your hand be with them Lord and bring them home safely. Father I come against every predator and kidnapper, those who would prey on young children and decree and declare that their plans are spoiled right now in the name of Jesus. I call for Michael the archangel, Your heavenly host and Your warring angels to come forth and protect all the missing children from every arrow and dart of evil right now in Jesus name, Amen.

DAY 32 – PEER PRESSURE

God has called us to follow His way and His word. There will be times when following the Lord will place you in a position where no one will share your opinion, but God. Will you do the right thing and obey the Lord God, or will you fold and bow to peer pressure, popularity or whatever is considered politically correct? God has called you to be the salt of the earth, not to hold up the status quo. You are in the world, but not of the world, so don't be afraid of being singled out as different. Don't follow the crowd, join the gang or embrace the mob's mentality. Everyone will not like you no matter what you do, so just demand their respect and concern yourself with pleasing God, not man. Heaven and Earth shall pass away, and in the end, only what you do for Christ will last. Be a LEADER and lead and draw your friends, family and love ones to Christ. Don't follow today's worldly trends and styles, create your own. Be different, be set apart for such a time as this.

Exodus 23:1-3 [1] You shall not repeat *or* raise a false report; you shall not join with the wicked to be an unrighteous witness. [2] You shall not follow a crowd to do evil; nor shall you bear witness at a trial so as to side with a multitude to pervert justice. [3] Neither shall you be partial to a poor man in his trial [just because he is poor] (AMP).

Judges 2:11-13 [11] And the people of Israel did evil in the sight of the Lord and served the Baals. [12] And they forsook the Lord, the God of their fathers, Who brought them out of the land of Egypt. They went after other gods of the peoples round about them and bowed down to them, and provoked the Lord to anger. [13] And they forsook the Lord and served Baal [the god worshiped by the Canaanites] and the Ashtaroth [female deities such as Ashtoreth and Asherah] (AMP).

Luke 23:13-25 [13] Pilate then called together the chief priests and the rulers and the people, [14] And said to them, You brought this Man before me as One Who was perverting *and* misleading *and* [a]turning away *and* corrupting the people;

and behold, after examining Him before you, I have not found any offense (crime or guilt) in this Man in regard to your accusations against Him; [15] No, nor indeed did Herod, for he sent Him back to us; behold, He has done nothing deserving of death. [16] I will therefore chastise Him *and* [b]deliver Him amended (reformed, taught His lesson) and release Him. [17] [c]*For it was necessary for him to release to them one prisoner at the Feast.* [18] But they all together raised a deep cry [from the depths of their throats], saying, Away with this Man! Release to us Barabbas! [19] He was a man who had been thrown into prison for raising a riot in the city, and for murder. [20] Once more Pilate called to them, wishing to release Jesus; [21] But they kept shouting out, Crucify, crucify Him! [22] A third time he said to them, Why? What wrong has He done? I have found [no offense or crime or guilt] in Him nothing deserving of death; I will therefore chastise Him [[d]in order to teach Him better] and release Him. [23] But they were insistent *and* urgent, demanding with loud cries that He should be crucified. And their voices prevailed (accomplished their purpose). [24] And Pilate gave sentence, that what they asked should be done. [25] So he released the man who had been thrown into prison for riot and murder, for whom they continued to ask, but Jesus he delivered up to be done with as they willed (AMP).

Though Pilate, found not fault in Jesus, he gave in to pressure from the Jewish people. He chastised Jesus, believing that the people would be appeased, however they demanded the release of Barabbas, instead of Jesus.

Prayer

God of the Breakthrough, the One who sets examples that others follow, bless Your children to not be turned by pressure from peers, nor pressures from the world. Let them not slide back into the old ways of the pass, but forward into the blessed life with You. Bless them to be comfortable in the skin that they are in as believers of the Lord. Bless them to be trend setters and not followers doing anything just to fit into the crowd, to blend in and not be set apart. Bless them to be the salt of the Earth and not lose their flavor. Bless them to continue to press their way and push and praise their way through to You, in Jesus name I pray, Amen.

DAY 33 – KIDNAPPED CHILDREN

Kidnapping is a crime punishable by law. In our recent news we heard about an Ohio woman and her child being kidnapped and held captive. We hear many news reports and stories about children who have been kidnapped and we find that the majority of the time, it's a family member. Sometimes it's an estranged parent who has lost their parental rights through separation and divorce. There are other times, however when the other parent just doesn't want to share custody of the child/ren. Joseph's brothers sold him into slavery. They were tired of the dreamer and also jealous of the attention given by their father Jacob to their younger brother Joseph. Joseph was the son of Jacob's old age and the first son born to him through his union with his beloved wife Rachael.

Genesis 37:17-28 [17] And the man said, They are departed hence; for I heard them say, Let us go to Dothan. And Joseph went after his brethren, and found them in Dothan. [18] And when they saw him afar off, even before he came near unto them, they conspired against him to slay him. [19] And they said one to another, Behold, this dreamer cometh. [20] Come now therefore, and let us slay him, and cast him into some pit, and we will say, Some evil beast hath devoured him: and we shall see what will become of his dreams. [21] And Reuben heard it, and he delivered him out of their hands; and said, Let us not kill him. [22] And Reuben said unto them, Shed no blood, but cast him into this pit that is in the wilderness, and lay no hand upon him; that he might rid him out of their hands, to deliver him to his father again. [23] And it came to pass, when Joseph was come unto his brethren, that they stript Joseph out of his coat, his coat of many colours that was on him; [24] And they took him, and cast him into a pit: and the pit was empty, there was no water in it. [25] And they sat down to eat bread: and they lifted up their eyes and looked, and, behold, a company of Ishmeelites came from Gilead with their camels bearing spicery and balm and myrrh, going to carry it down to Egypt. [26] And Judah said unto his brethren, What profit is it if we slay our brother, and conceal his blood? [27] Come, and let us sell him to the Ishmeelites, and let not our hand be upon him; for he is our brother and our flesh. And his brethren were content. [28] Then there passed by Midianites merchantmen; and they drew and lifted up Joseph out of the pit, and sold Joseph to the Ishmeelites for twenty pieces of silver: and they brought Joseph into Egypt (KJV).

Prayer

Heavenly Father, heavenly King, Lord You who are our Place of Refuge, our Rock our Shield our Sword our Protector from all hurt and harm, bless Your sweet, adorable and holy name. You are the Lilly of the Valley and the Rose of Sharon, a wise and wonderful Counselor, the bright and Morning Star, the Bread of Life, Lover, Savior and Redeemer of our souls. Bless Lord, protect and keep all those children who have been kidnapped for whatever reason or purpose. Lord let no hurt or harm come to them. Bless them to know that You are there for them and that You have not forsaken them. Use their situation Lord to show you Glory. Let it work for Your good Lord, in Jesus name, we pray, Amen.

DAY 34 – SEX TRADE TRAFFICKING CHILDREN

In the Old Testament there were people who lived around Israel that God detested. They offered their children as sacrifices to gods and God wiped many of them out for these awful practices. Today there are some parents and adults who will take advantage of children and use them and sell them for others sexual pleasures. Many missing children are caught up in this trade, abused and misused. Plead the blood of Jesus over the children and those who would wrongfully use them in this manner. Just a few months ago, there were 3 young women who had been taken in their teens by a man in Cleveland and held approximately 10 years. They were used as sex slaves and one had a child born in that situation. Just yesterday there was a story in the news of an Ohio woman and her child held captive for 2 years in Ashland, Ohio by 3 people. They threatened the woman and her child with pit bulls and snakes. Though the woman was disabled she and her child were beaten and forced to work while in captivity.

Deuteronomy 18:9-10 ⁹ When thou art come into the land which the LORD thy God giveth thee, thou shalt not learn to do after the abominations of those nations. ¹⁰ There shall not be found among you any one that maketh his son or his daughter to pass through the fire, or that useth divination, or an observer of times, or an enchanter, or a witch.

Prayer

Father I plead the blood of Jesus over all the children who will be stolen and those who will fall into the hands of mischievous adults who will sell and use them in the sex trade. Have mercy upon the children who are held captive against their wills oh Lord. Protect them and help them to escape these traps of bondage. Bring justice into their lives and punish those who have violated them and done them harm, in Jesus name, I pray, Amen.

DAY 35 – ORPHANS

In many nations and foreign lands children are unwanted, their parents are too poor to provide for them or one or both of their parents are dead. Some are in nations where there has been a large population of untreated HIV and AIDS and their parents died and left them homeless at a very early age. And there are even other nations where children once they reach the age of 16 are put out of their parent's home. Whatever the case they find themselves as orphans, motherless and/or fatherless. Although America is still a rich nation overall, we also have orphaned children.

Deuteronomy 10:18 ¹⁸ He doth execute the judgment of the fatherless and widow, and loveth the stranger, in giving him food and raiment (KJV).

James 1:27 External religious worship [religion as it is expressed in outward acts] that is pure and unblemished in the sight of God the Father is this: to visit and help and care for the orphans and widows in their affliction and need, and to keep oneself unspotted and uncontaminated from the world (AMP).

Prayer

Heavenly Father, in the name of Jesus, hallowed be Your great and mighty name. Lord You are Alpha and Omega, the Beginning and the End. You're a Father to the fatherless and a Mother to the motherless. You care for those that some have cast away and cast out, You love the unlovable ones. Some of your children may find themselves on a doorstep abandoned by their biological parents, even left for dead. But You oh Lord are faithful and You never leave us nor forsake us, You are a present help in the times of trouble and You are there meeting our needs. Thank You Lord for showing us Your compassion and Your unconditional love. Thank You Lord for being our Everything. Lord You said there would always be poor among us, bless those who are orphans, poor and homeless, according to Your riches in glory, meet their every need Lord. Jehovah Jirah You are our Provider and our Source, bless the orphans and those who are in need with food and shelter and someone who will love and care for them. Lord bless that they not be mistreated, but cared for and given dignity and respect in Jesus name I pray Amen.

PRAYER TARGETS AND PERSONAL NOTES

_____

_____

_____

_____

_____

_____

_____

_____

_____

_____

_____

_____

_____

_____

_____

_____

_____

_____

_____

_____

_____

_____

_____

_____

_____

_____

_____

_____

_____

_____

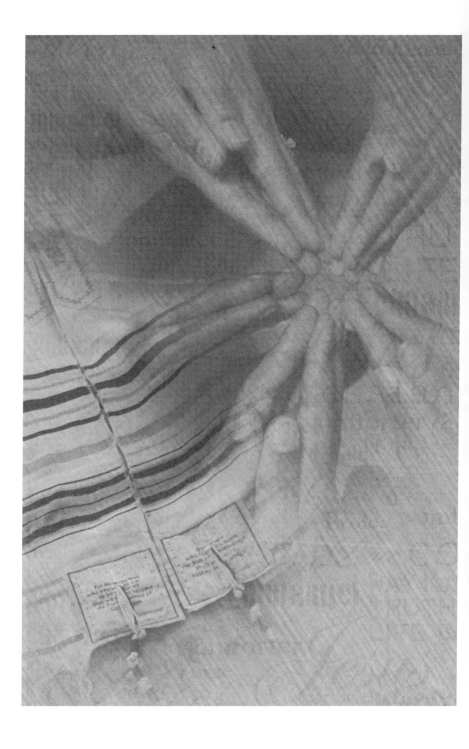

SECTION IV

EXTENDED FAMILY MEMBERS

DAY 36 – COUSINS

I am one of 10 children that the Lord blessed my parents with and though my parents went on to have many, many grandchildren, great grandchildren and even a great, great grandchild before my father died; many of us have only 1 child or just 2 children. In the second generation of the children of George and Myrtle Smith the first cousins have relationship with their cousins who are to them their sisters and brothers. The bonds that unite them together are strong. In the word we can find examples of both good and bad influences from our cousins upon each other. A poor example of a relationship with a cousin comes from 2 Samuel 13:3-4 in which Jonadab gave ill advice to his cousin Amnon. The advice that he gave Amnon was a terrible scheme to get his sister, Tamar to come into his room so that he could rape her.

> **2 Samuel 13:3-6** [3] But Amnon had a friend, whose name was Jonadab, the son of Shimeah David's brother: and Jonadab was a very subtil man. [4] And he said unto him, Why art thou, being the king's son, lean from day to day? wilt thou not tell me? And Amnon said unto him, I love Tamar, my brother Absalom's sister. [5] And Jonadab said unto him, Lay thee down on thy bed,

and make thyself sick: and when thy father cometh to see thee, say unto him, I pray thee, let my sister Tamar come, and give me meat, and dress the meat in my sight, that I may see it, and eat it at her hand. ⁶ So Amnon lay down, and made himself sick: and when the king was come to see him, Amnon said unto the king, I pray thee, let Tamar my sister come, and make me a couple of cakes in my sight, that I may eat at her hand (KJV).

Unfortunately for Amnon he followed this ill advice which later caused him to lose his life (See 2 Samuel 13:23-39).

The relationship between Elizabeth and Mary was a good one and an interesting one. One woman was older in age and the birth of her son was a long awaited one. The other was almost married and was impregnated by the Holy Spirit, it was a virgin birth. They were both pregnant with excitement for the sons that were yet coming. Both their sons would die at a young age, having fulfilled what the Lord God had purposed for their lives. Elizabeth's son John started his ministry first and actually prepared the way for Jesus's ministry.

Luke 1:23-28 ²³ And it came to pass, that, as soon as the days of his ministration were accomplished, he departed to his own house. ²⁴ And after those days his wife Elisabeth conceived, and hid herself five months, saying, ²⁵ Thus hath the Lord dealt with me in the days wherein he looked on me, to take away my reproach among men. ²⁶ And in the sixth month the angel Gabriel was sent from God unto a city of Galilee, named Nazareth, ²⁷ To a virgin espoused to a man whose name was Joseph, of the house of David; and the virgin's name was Mary. ²⁸ And the angel came in unto her, and said, Hail, thou that art highly favoured, the Lord is with thee: blessed art thou among women (KJV).

Luke 1: 29-44 ²⁹ And when she saw him, she was troubled at his saying, and cast in her mind what manner of salutation this should be. ³⁰ And the angel said unto her, Fear not, Mary: for thou hast found favour with God. ³¹ And, behold, thou shalt conceive in thy womb, and bring forth a son, and shalt call his name Jesus. ³² He shall be great, and shall be called the Son of the

Highest: and the Lord God shall give unto him the throne of his father David: ³³ And he shall reign over the house of Jacob for ever; and of his kingdom there shall be no end. ³⁴ Then said Mary unto the angel, How shall this be, seeing I know not a man? ³⁵ And the angel answered and said unto her, The Holy Ghost shall come upon thee, and the power of the Highest shall overshadow thee: therefore also that holy thing which shall be born of thee shall be called the Son of God. ³⁶ And, behold, thy cousin Elisabeth, she hath also conceived a son in her old age: and this is the sixth month with her, who was called barren. ³⁷ For with God nothing shall be impossible. ³⁸ And Mary said, Behold the handmaid of the Lord; be it unto me according to thy word. And the angel departed from her. ³⁹ And Mary arose in those days, and went into the hill country with haste, into a city of Judah; ⁴⁰ And entered into the house of Zacharias, and saluted Elisabeth. ⁴¹ And it came to pass, that, when Elisabeth heard the salutation of Mary, the babe leaped in her womb; and Elisabeth was filled with the Holy Ghost: ⁴² And she spake out with a loud voice, and said, Blessed art thou among women, and blessed is the fruit of thy womb. ⁴³ And whence is this to me, that the mother of my Lord should come to me? ⁴⁴ For, lo, as soon as the voice of thy salutation sounded in mine ears, the babe leaped in my womb for joy (KJV).

The relationship between John the Baptist and Jesus was unique. John was allowed to prepare the way for his cousin Jesus. Look at the following scriptures of how God used them for one another.

Matthew 3:1-6 In those days came John the Baptist, preaching in the wilderness of Judaea, ² And saying, Repent ye: for the kingdom of heaven is at hand. ³ For this is he that was spoken of by the prophet Esaias, saying, The voice of one crying in the wilderness, Prepare ye the way of the Lord, make his paths straight. ⁴ And the same John had his raiment of camel's hair, and a leathern girdle about his loins; and his meat was locusts and wild honey. ⁵ Then went out to him Jerusalem, and all Judaea, and all the region round about Jordan, ⁶ And were baptized of him in Jordan, confessing their sins (KJV).

Matthew 3:13-15 [13] Then cometh Jesus from Galilee to Jordan unto John, to be baptized of him. [14] But John forbad him, saying, I have need to be baptized of thee, and comest thou to me? [15] And Jesus answering said unto him, Suffer it to be so now: for thus it becometh us to fulfil all righteousness. Then he suffered him (KJV).

Matthew 11:11 [1] Verily I say unto you, Among them that are born of women there hath not risen a greater than John the Baptist: notwithstanding he that is least in the kingdom of heaven is greater than he (KJV).

John 3:25-36 [25] Then there arose a question between some of John's disciples and the Jews about purifying. [26] And they came unto John, and said unto him, Rabbi, he that was with thee beyond Jordan, to whom thou barest witness, behold, the same baptizeth, and all men come to him. [27] John answered and said, A man can receive nothing, except it be given him from heaven. [28] Ye yourselves bear me witness, that I said, I am not the Christ, but that I am sent before him. [29] He that hath the bride is the bridegroom: but the friend of the bridegroom, which standeth and heareth him, rejoiceth greatly because of the bridegroom's voice: this my joy therefore is fulfilled. [30] He must increase, but I must decrease. [31] He that cometh from above is above all: he that is of the earth is earthly, and speaketh of the earth: he that cometh from heaven is above all. [32] And what he hath seen and heard, that he testifieth; and no man receiveth his testimony. [33] He that hath received his testimony hath set to his seal that God is true. [34] For he whom God hath sent speaketh the words of God: for God giveth not the Spirit by measure unto him. [35] The Father loveth the Son, and hath given all things into his hand. [36] He that believeth on the Son hath everlasting life: and he that believeth not the Son shall not see life; but the wrath of God abideth on him (KJV).

Prayer

God of love, God of mercy and God of grace, in the name of Jesus, I give You glory. Truly You are the One and only Wise God. I thank You Lord for You have placed within our own families cousins who are like our own sisters and

brothers. They are a bond of love and a bond of friendship for some likened to the relationship of Mary and Elizabeth and David and Jonathan. Bless us Lord to have a good influence on our family members, our cousins the children of our parents siblings and the generations that follow. Let us have loving and kind relationships that push and propel one another forward into greatness, like John and Jesus. Help us not to lead one another astray like Jonadab led Amnon. Allow us to bless each other and joy in the accomplishments of one another. Let us offer a helping hand to each other and share our life experiences like sisters and brothers, in Jesus name, Amen.

DAY 37 – IN LAWS – OUTLAWS

Scripture provides good examples of in-laws like Jethro (Moses' father-in-law, Exodus 18) and Naomi (Ruth's mother-in-law, Ruth Chapters 1-4). But then there are others whom I am referring to as outlaws like Aaron and Meriam who didn't like Moses' wife who was not Jewish, but a woman of color a Midianite. God punished them for that and rebelling against Moses. Then there was the king, Herod Antipas whom John the Baptist verbally chastised who married his brother Philip's wife, Herodia and the brother was not dead you'll (Matthew 14:1-11; Mark 6:16-28; Luke 3:19, 20).

Just as there is a role for parents, siblings and other relatives, when one in your family is married, first get to know their spouses and their family. Don't judge and disrespect them, get to know your in-laws. If they show themselves to be of poor character, pray and ask God for guidance, let Him help and intercede in the matter. Don't take things into your own hands first to straighten out and to meddle.

Exodus 18:13-24 [13] And it came to pass on the morrow, that Moses sat to judge the people: and the people stood by Moses from the morning unto the evening. [14] And when Moses' father in law saw all that he did to the people, he said, What is this thing that thou doest to the people? why sittest thou thyself alone, and all the people stand by thee from morning unto even? [15] And Moses said unto his father in law, Because the people come unto me to enquire of God: [16] When they have a matter, they come unto me; and I judge between one and another, and I do make them know the statutes of God, and his laws. [17] And Moses' father in law said unto him, The thing that thou doest is not good. [18] Thou wilt surely wear away, both thou, and this people that is with thee: for this thing is too heavy for thee; thou art not able to perform it thyself alone. [19] Hearken now unto my voice, I will give thee counsel, and God shall be with thee: Be thou for the people to God-ward, that thou mayest bring the causes unto God: [20] And thou shalt teach them ordinances and laws, and shalt shew them the way wherein they must walk, and the work that they must do. [21] Moreover thou shalt provide out of all the people able men, such as fear God, men of truth, hating covetousness; and place such over them, to be rulers of thousands, and rulers of hundreds, rulers of fifties, and rulers of tens: [22] And let them judge the people at all seasons: and it shall be, that every great matter they shall bring unto thee, but every small matter they shall judge: so shall it be easier for thyself, and they shall bear the burden with thee. [23] If thou shalt do this thing, and God command thee so, then thou shalt be able to endure, and all this people shall also go to their place in peace. [24] So Moses hearkened to the voice of his father in law, and did all that he had said (KJV).

Jethro provided Moses with wise counsel. Moses had been carrying the weight of judging and counseling the entire nation of Israel. These tasks alone, could have possibly killed him had he not taken the good instruction given to him by his father-in-law, Jethro. Teaching others the laws and ordinances and delegating authority to them to make judgment decisions lightened the load of Moses and also allowed him to deal with the more serious matters.

In the book of Ruth (Ruth Chapter 1), Naomi, her husband and 2 sons went to Moab because there was a famine in Judah. Her husband died and her 2 sons married Moabite women (Orpah and Ruth) and after 10 years both sons died. Naomi must have been a great mother-in-law for the 2 daughter-in-laws both wanted to go with her when she decided to depart from Moab. Naomi heard that the Lord had blessed Judah with a harvest again.

Ruth 1:11-17 [11] And Naomi said, Turn again, my daughters: why will ye go with me? are there yet any more sons in my womb, that they may be your husbands? [12] Turn again, my daughters, go your way; for I am too old to have an husband. If I should say, I have hope, if I should have an husband also to night, and should also bear sons; [13] Would ye tarry for them till they were grown? would ye stay for them from having husbands? nay, my daughters; for it grieveth me much for your sakes that the hand of the LORD is gone out against me. [14] And they lifted up their voice, and wept again: and Orpah kissed her mother in law; but Ruth clave unto her. [15] And she said, Behold, thy sister in law is gone back unto her people, and unto her gods: return thou after thy sister in law. [16] And Ruth said, Intreat me not to leave thee, or to return from following after thee: for whither thou goest, I will go; and where thou lodgest, I will lodge: thy people shall be my people, and thy God my God: [17] Where thou diest, will I die, and there will I be buried: the LORD do so to me, and more also, if ought but death part thee and me (KJV).

They arrive into Judah and though Naomi tried to convince Ruth to stay in Moab, we find her still leading her daughter-in-law and helping her.

Ruth 3:1-6 [1] Then Naomi her mother in law said unto her, My daughter, shall I not seek rest for thee, that it may be well with thee? [2] And now is not Boaz of our kindred, with whose maidens thou wast? Behold, he winnoweth barley to night in the threshing floor. [3] Wash thyself therefore, and anoint thee, and put thy raiment upon thee, and get thee down to the floor: but make not thyself known unto the man, until he shall have done eating and drinking. [4] And it shall be, when he lieth down, that thou shalt mark the place where he shall lie, and thou shalt go in, and uncover his feet, and lay thee down; and he will tell thee what thou shalt do. [5] And she said unto her, All that thou sayest unto me I will do. [6] And she went down unto the floor, and did according to all that her mother in law bade her.

In the scripture below, we can tell immediately that Miriam and Aaron are not pleased and are unhappy with their sister-in-law. In fact, they opened up their mouths and spoke ill of Moses, because they did not like his choice of spouse. Additionally, we even see that there is some jealously and sibling rivalry.

Numbers 12:1-9 [1]And Miriam and Aaron spake against Moses because of the Ethiopian woman whom he had married: for he had married an Ethiopian woman. [2] And they said, Hath the LORD indeed spoken only by Moses? hath he not spoken also by us? And the LORD heard it. [3] (Now the man Moses was very meek, above all the men which were upon the face of the earth.) [4] And the LORD spake suddenly unto Moses, and unto Aaron, and unto Miriam, Come out ye three unto the tabernacle of the congregation. And they three came out. [5] And the LORD came down in the pillar of the cloud, and stood in the door of the tabernacle, and called Aaron and Miriam: and they both came forth. [6] And he said, Hear now my words: If there be a prophet among you, I the LORD will make myself known unto him in a vision, and will speak unto him in a dream. [7] My servant Moses is not so, who is faithful in all mine house. [8] With him will I speak mouth to mouth, even apparently, and not in dark speeches; and the similitude of the LORD shall he behold: wherefore then were ye not afraid to speak against my servant Moses? [9] And the anger of the LORD was kindled against them; and he departed (KJV).

Prayer

Heavenly Father, Giver of our heritage, which is our children, in Jesus name, thank You for our children. Lord just as we have given our children to You, bless us to release them and be a blessing to their new spouses. Bless us to be a blessing and not a hindrance. Bless us to be good and pleasant in laws, and not act like outlaws. Lord let us not take sides and brew mess. Help us be wise counselors when our advice is requested and not add our 2 cents worth or give out a piece of our minds. Let us not meddle, gossip, intrude or interfere but bless, uplift, encourage and bridle our tongues, in Jesus name, I pray, Amen.

DAY 38 – WIDOWS AND WIDOWERS

In the Old Testament we find where the Lord taught that we are to take care of widows and orphans. You also find that He speaks to us about providing for the poor. Many times it's the widows who will find themselves in need of something that is easy to give and that is love. They along with orphans will often be highly represented in the population that makes up the poor in our lands. In particular, the widows are another group of individuals that we should target to bless and to lift up in prayer.

Exodus 22:22 [22] Ye shall not afflict any widow, or fatherless child (KJV).

Psalm 146:9 [9] The LORD preserveth the strangers; he relieveth the fatherless and widow: but the way of the wicked he turneth upside down (KJV).

1 Timothy 5:3 [3] Honour widows that are widows indeed (KJV).

Prayer

Lord, You are the Light and the Life of all man, and Provider of all, Jehovah Jireh. You are also, The Bread of Life and the One who feeds our spirits and souls. In the name of Jesus, You have instructed us to care for the elders, especially those who are widows indeed. Many of them have no one but You Lord. Bless them today Lord with food, shelter and clothing. Let them not be homeless Father, nor on the street begging for bread. Provide their every need Lord, according to Your riches in Glory, be it done unto them, in Jesus name, I pray, Amen.

PRAYER TARGETS AND PERSONAL NOTES

_____
_____
_____
_____
_____
_____
_____
_____
_____
_____
_____
_____
_____
_____
_____
_____
_____
_____
_____
_____
_____
_____
_____
_____
_____
_____
_____
_____

_____
_____
_____
_____
_____
_____
_____
_____
_____
_____
_____
_____
_____
_____
_____
_____
_____
_____
_____
_____
_____
_____
_____
_____
_____
_____
_____
_____
_____
_____
_____

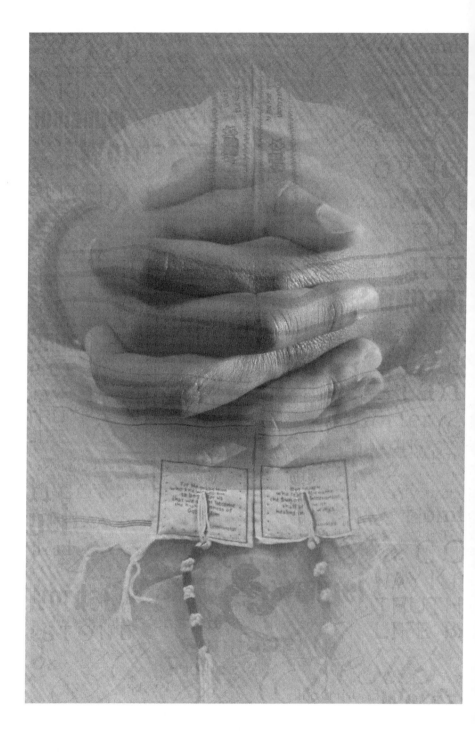

MARRIAGES

DAY 39 – MARRIAGES

It is God who ordained marriage and blessed it to be a holy union between a man and a woman. He made the two to become one flesh. The two that He has joined to be one, He has said let not man pull apart. He said that he who finds a wife, finds a good thing and is blessed of the Lord. A marriage begins with a wedding and vows are taken as the 2 parties commit themselves one to the other. Traditional marriage vows are still used more now than personalized ones. I, (name), take you (name), to be my lawfully wedded (husband, wife), to have and to hold from this day forward, for better or for worse, for richer, for poorer, in sickness and in health, to love and to cherish: from this day forward until death do us part. And whereas most of us are excited and happy to recite these vows on our wedding day, what we see in America today is 6 of 10 marriages ending in divorce. That's across the board you'll, even in the church.

When the challenges of life come along, let us not forget the vows that we made to one another. When or if a spouse loses a job, and the other spouse has to go into the workforce or carry the load alone, remember the words you spoke, for richer or for poorer. If one is in an accident and is disabled or stricken with an illness or disease, don't leave them, remember you said, "In sickness and in health." When you get older and the fire is not what it used to be, don't rush out looking for someone else to light your flame, remember you said, "To love and to cherish: from this day forward until death do us part." Perhaps you need to renew your vows annually on your anniversary to recall your vows back into your conscious memory. You might need to renew them monthly, weekly or even daily. The point being made here is to give your marriage a chance to work, fight for it, remember your commitment and the vows you made. The devil came to kill, steal and destroy and that includes your marriage. Pray and ask God to help you keep Him first and keep your marriage alive, on one accord and in unity and in peace with one another. All jokes aside, if or when you find that your spouse was deceptive and only showed you their representative during the dating process, and you find your marriage is unequally yoked, seek counseling first. Let separation and divorce be a last resort. If there are children involved, go the extra mile or even more to work things out. Children lives are so impressionable and precious; give them the opportunity to have a good family life and home.

Matthew 19:4-6 [4] And he answered and said unto them, Have ye not read, that he which made them at the beginning made them male and female, [5] And said, For this cause shall a man leave father and mother, and shall cleave to his wife: and they twain shall be one flesh? [6] Wherefore they are no more twain, but one flesh. What therefore God hath joined together, let not man put asunder (KJV).

Hebrews 13:4 [4] Let marriage be held in honor (esteemed worthy, precious, of great price, and especially dear) in all things. And thus let the marriage bed be undefiled (kept undishonored); for God will judge and punish the unchaste [all guilty of sexual vice] and adulterous (AMP).

Prayer

Lord bless our marriages to be kind and harmonious relationships that are fruitful and a blessing to You. Bless our marriages to be unions where children are raised knowing You Lord and following Your ways. Let all marriages be between one man and one woman and let there be no wondering eyes or straying hearts, in the name of Jesus. Let the women be found Lord and show them how to wait, bless them with Your grace. Bless all Your children to marry the spouses that You have chosen for them in Jesus name. Bless the husbands and wives to be at peace with one another and united on one accord as in Your original plan. Lord, when there is divorce, where there is separation, bless the married couples to still show brotherly love and not seek to hurt, harm and destroy each other in Jesus name, we pray, Amen.

DAY 40 – SAME SEX MARRIAGES

In the beginning God made woman for man and man for woman. He did not call like genders to come together as one, and His word is unchanging, He has not changed His mind. Current trends and worldly practices are adopting alternative lifestyles for gays and lesbians to marry, but God did not command it to be so. What He did say is that we should love one another. So we don't adopt or condone their lifestyle practices, but we do show them love. We don't have to agree with those who believe in same sex marriage, in fact, we can agree to disagree and still show love. We don't make fun of them or target them for mischief, but we must pray for them. They can be delivered, though it may be very difficult, because they have become soul ties. Soul ties are difficult to break, however nothing is impossible for God.

Genesis 1:26-28 [26] And God said, Let us make man in our image, after our likeness: and let them have dominion over the fish of the sea, and over the fowl of the air, and over the cattle, and over all the earth, and over every creeping thing that creepeth upon the earth. [27] So God created man in his own image, in the image of God created he him; male and female created he them. [28] And God blessed them, and God said unto them, Be fruitful, and multiply, and replenish the earth, and subdue it: and have dominion over the fish of the sea, and over the fowl of the air, and over every living thing that moveth upon the earth (KJV).

Genesis 2:21-24 [21] And the LORD God caused a deep sleep to fall upon Adam, and he slept: and he took one of his ribs, and closed up the flesh instead thereof; [22] And the rib, which the LORD God had taken from man, made he a woman, and brought her unto the man. [23] And Adam said, This is now bone of my bones, and flesh of my flesh: she shall be called Woman, because she was taken out of Man. [24] Therefore shall a man leave his father and his mother, and shall cleave unto his wife: and they shall be one flesh (KJV).

Leviticus 18:22 [22] Do not have sexual relations with a man as one does with a woman, that is detestable (NIV).

Leviticus 20:13 [13] If a man lie with mankind, as he lieth with a woman, both of them have committed an abomination….(KJV).

Prayer

Heavenly Father, in the name of Jesus, you created the husband for the wife and made a marriage between one woman and one man. Society may attempt to change this, but Your word does not change Lord, it is the same yesterday, today and tomorrow and it does not return to you void, but accomplishes all that you set it out to do. Bless us Lord to know the truth that sets us free and the difference between the tricks, lies and schemes of the devil which says it ain't so. Let us not defile our bodies which are the temple of the Holy Spirit. Bless us to be obedient, that the man leaves his father and mother and cleaves unto his wife, in Jesus name I pray, Amen.

PRAYER TARGETS AND PERSONAL NOTES

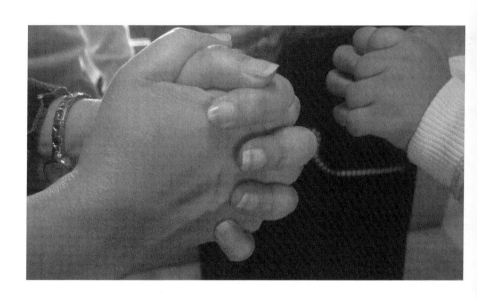

SECTION VI

FAMILY ISSUES

DAY 41 – SEPARATION & DIVORCE

Because separation in a marriage pulls apart the union that God has brought together, separation and divorce should not be taken lightly. Marriage vows should be taken seriously and one should not go into marriage saying well if this doesn't work out, I'll just get a divorce. There are times and situations that occur that may pull a marriage apart. Adultery and physical violence contribute to separation and divorce and God has not called us to either. Some situations are resolved through marriage counseling. While I don't advise a spouse to remain in an abusive situation, I do encourage couples to start a relationship with God at the center of both of their lives. Take the time to get to know one another first, and be sure to pray and ask God, is this the one that He has set aside for you as your spouse. He will help you to separate from your emotions and listen to His voice of wisdom.

Matthew 19:7-9 [7] They say unto him, Why did Moses then command to give a writing of divorcement, and to put her away? [8] He saith unto them, Moses because of the hardness of your hearts suffered you to put away your wives: but from the beginning it was not so. [9] And I say unto you, Whosoever shall put away his wife, except it be for fornication, and shall marry another, committeth adultery: and whoso marrieth her which is put away doth commit adultery (KJV).

Malachi 2:16 ¹⁶For the Lord, the God of Israel, says: I hate divorce and marital separation and him who covers his garment [his wife] with violence. Therefore keep a watch upon your spirit [that it may be controlled by My Spirit], that you deal not treacherously and faithlessly [with your marriage mate] (AMP).

1 Corinthians 7:1-16 ¹Now concerning the things whereof ye wrote unto me: It is good for a man not to touch a woman. ²Nevertheless, to avoid fornication, let every man have his own wife, and let every woman have her own husband. ³Let the husband render unto the wife due benevolence: and likewise also the wife unto the husband. ⁴The wife hath not power of her own body, but the husband: and likewise also the husband hath not power of his own body, but the wife. ⁵Defraud ye not one the other, except it be with consent for a time, that ye may give yourselves to fasting and prayer; and come together again, that Satan tempt you not for your incontinency. ⁶But I speak this by permission, and not of commandment. ⁷For I would that all men were even as I myself. But every man hath his proper gift of God, one after this manner, and another after that. ⁸I say therefore to the unmarried and widows, it is good for them if they abide even as I. ⁹But if they cannot contain, let them marry: for it is better to marry than to burn. ¹⁰And unto the married I command, yet not I, but the Lord, Let not the wife depart from her husband: ¹¹But and if she depart, let her remain unmarried or be reconciled to her husband: and let not the husband put away his wife. ¹²But to the rest speak I, not the Lord: If any brother hath a wife that believeth not, and she be pleased to dwell with him, let him not put her away. ¹³And the woman which hath an husband that believeth not, and if he be pleased to dwell with her, let her not leave him. ¹⁴For the unbelieving husband is sanctified by the wife, and the unbelieving wife is sanctified by the husband: else were your children unclean; but now are they holy. ¹⁵But if the unbelieving depart, let him depart. A brother or a sister is not under bondage in such cases: but God hath called us to peace. ¹⁶For what knowest thou, O wife, whether thou shalt save thy husband? or how knowest thou, O man, whether thou shalt save thy wife (KJV)?

Prayer

Gracious Lord You said what You have joined together, let no one set asunder. Lord I pull down strongholds, misunderstandings, chaos and confusion, miscommunications, disunity, deceit, discord and everything that would break up marriages. I command separation and divorce to dry up and I caste them to dry places in the name of Jesus. I command walls and barriers that have stood in the way of agreement to fall and crumble now in the name of Jesus. I ask You to strengthen marriages right now in the name of Jesus. Bless husbands and wives to stay together in unity on one accord until death do they part, in Jesus name, Amen. Halleluiah!

DAY 42 – DOMESTIC VIOLENCE

Domestic violence is one-on-one, up close and personal. It's our spouses, partners, children, those that we are closest to that really suffer. They are observers, perpetrators and sometimes victims, and in the worse cases unfortunately sometimes they are the DOAs (Dead on Arrival). A hot temper, too much to drink, a pattern of abuse from one generation to another is the culprit, but it is not the will of God. Man's inhumanity to man is on the rise and wounding our families. With the help of God we can stop it!

Psalms 11:5 [5]The Lord tests the righteous and the wicked, And the one who loves violence His soul hates (NAS).

Colossians 3:19 [19]Husbands, love your wives, and do not be harsh with them (ESV).

2 Timothy 3:1-5 [1]But understand this, that in the last days there will come times of difficulty. [2]For people will be lovers of self, lovers of money, proud, arrogant, abusive, disobedient to their parents, ungrateful, unholy, [3] heartless, unappeasable, slanderous, without self-control, brutal, not loving good, [4] treacherous, reckless, swollen with conceit, lovers of pleasure rather than lovers of God, [5] having the appearance of godliness, but denying its power. Avoid such people (ESV).

1 Peter 3:7 [7] Likewise, husbands, live with your wives in an understanding way, showing honor to the woman as the weaker vessel, since they are heirs with you of the grace of life, so that your prayers may not be hindered (ESV).

1 Corinthians 13:4-7 [4] Love is patient and kind; love does not envy or boast; it is not arrogant [5] or rude. It does not insist on its own way; it is not irritable or resentful;[a] [6] it does not rejoice at wrongdoing, but rejoices with the truth. [7] Love bears all things, believes all things, hopes all things, endures all things (ESV).

Galatians 5:19-21 [19] Now the works of the flesh are evident: sexual immorality, impurity, sensuality, [20] idolatry, sorcery, enmity, strife, jealousy, fits of anger, rivalries, dissensions, divisions, [21] envy,[a] drunkenness, orgies, and things like these. I warn you, as I warned you before, that those who do such things will not inherit the kingdom of God (ESV).

Ephesians 4:29-32 [29] Let no corrupting talk come out of your mouths, but only such as is good for building up, as fits the occasion, that it may give grace to those who hear. [30] And do not grieve the Holy Spirit of God, by whom you were sealed for the day of redemption. [31] Let all bitterness and wrath and anger and clamor and slander be put away from you, along with all malice. [32] Be kind to one another, tenderhearted, forgiving one another, as God in Christ forgave you (ESV).

Colossians 3:21 [21] Fathers, do not provoke your children, lest they become discouraged (ESV).

Romans 12:17-21 [17] Repay no one evil for evil, but give thought to do what is honorable in the sight of all. [18] If possible, so far as it depends on you, live peaceably with all. [19] Beloved, never avenge yourselves, but leave it[a] to the wrath of God, for it is written, "Vengeance is mine, I will repay, says the Lord." [20] To the contrary, "if your enemy is hungry, feed him; if he is thirsty, give him something to drink; for by so doing you will heap burning coals on his head." [21] Do not be overcome by evil, but overcome evil with good (ESV).

Prayer

Father You have called us to love and not to hate, to comfort and bring no harm. Bless us to be peace makers and not violent and abusive. Help us to communicate our differences and discuss them in love. Father we come against the spirit of anger and command it to go in the name of Jesus. We come against generational curses of abuse and domination and command them to dry up. We ask you Lord to lose Your perfect peace in its place in Jesus name. Lord bless us to live together in peace and harmony, to be stable in all our ways. Bless us to follow Your commands and receive Your instruction in Jesus name, Amen.

DAY 43 – GENERATIONAL CURSES – PRAYING AGAINST THEM

God warned men against polygamy. King David had many wives and a lot of half sons which brought a lot of dysfunction to his family. His son Solomon had many pagan wives and they turned his heart against God. 1 Kings 11:3 And he had seven hundred wives, princesses, and three hundred concubines: and his wives turned away his heart.

The sins of the fathers can pass on generational curses to their children and their children's children. The scripture below is 2 Samuel 16:21-22 fulfills the prophesy of Nathan that David's sin against Uriah (sleeping with his wife), that another man would sleep with David's wives.

2 Samuel 12:11-12 [11] Thus saith the LORD, Behold, I will raise up evil against thee out of thine own house, and I will take thy wives before thine eyes, and give them unto thy neighbour, and he shall lie with thy wives in the sight of this sun. [12] For thou didst it secretly: but I will do this thing before all Israel, and before the sun (KJV).

2 Samuel 16:21-22 [21] And Ahithophel said unto Absalom, Go in unto thy father's concubines, which he hath left to keep the house; and all Israel shall hear that thou art abhorred of thy father: then shall the hands of all that are with thee be strong. [22] So they spread Absalom a tent upon the top of the house; and Absalom went in unto his father's concubines in the sight of all Israel (KJV).

Prayer

Father God in the name of Jesus, You are an all knowing God. You know the many mistakes that we have made and we thank You for forgiving our sins and remembering them no more. Though we have already repented of our sins, we also cancel out the doors that we opened that would pass on curses throughout the generations of our seed. Bless our children to know You early in their lives and let them be led by Your Spirit and not their emotions in the name of Jesus. We cancel every plan and trap of the enemy against us and our seed. We repent for the sins of our elders and ourselves. We pull down all generational curses and cast them into the sea. Every weakness that the enemy discovered in us, he shall not be able to use against our children, in the name of Jesus. We decree and declare that no weapon formed against them shall prosper, in Jesus name. Father we employ Michael, Your archangel and Your heavenly host, Your warring angels to come forward and battle on behalf of our children, in Jesus name, Amen.

DAY 44 – JEALOUSY, ENVY, STRIFE: DON'T LET THEM SPOIL YOUR FAMILY

King David had several wives and many children (1 Chronicles Ch. 3) and there was turmoil within his family. One of the sons, Amnon falls in love with his sister Tamar who is the sister of Absalon (2 Samuel Ch. 13). Amnon lies to his father and says he is sick and ask for Tamar to come and cook for him. David sends Tamar to Amnon, he rapes her, then he detests her. King David did not discipline Amnon. Tamar goes to live with Absalon and 2 years later, Absolon kills his brother Amnon because of what he did to Tamar and then he flees. In 2 Samuel, Ch. 14 Absalon returns, but King David does not send him to prison, nor punish him, but will not allow him to see his face for 2 years. Absalon leads a rebellion against his own father, David in 2 Samuel Ch. 15 and David flees Jerusalem. Further on in Chapter 18 of 2 Samuel Absalon is killed by Joab, though King David had ordered that he not be killed.

Many families like that of King David are dysfunctional, rape, envy, strife, rebellion even murder existed within the family. As much as we love our children, we must discipline them. Perhaps if King David had taken some disciplinary action against his son Amnon, he possibly would not have lost 2 of his sons. The unfortunate rape of Tamar went unpunished by David and the ultimate results were ugly.

Many families are blended with step parents and step children, half-brothers and half-sisters. This may make the family unit and environment more challenging; however these families can operate without discord. There has to be respect in the household for the parents and the children. It may take some extra effort to live together in agreement, but all things are possible with God. We're not here to compete with one another, but to lift and encourage each other.

Proverbs 6:12-23 [12] A naughty person, a wicked man, walketh with a froward mouth. [13] He winketh with his eyes, he speaketh with his feet, he teacheth with his fingers; [14] Frowardness is in his heart, he deviseth mischief continually; he soweth discord. [15] Therefore shall his calamity come suddenly; suddenly shall he be broken without remedy. [16] These six things doth the LORD hate: yea, seven are an abomination unto him: [17] A proud look, a lying tongue, and hands that shed innocent blood, [18] An heart that deviseth wicked imaginations, feet that be swift in running to mischief, [19] A false witness that speaketh lies, and he that soweth discord among brethren. [20] My son, keep thy father's commandment, and forsake not the law of thy mother: [21] Bind them continually upon thine heart, and tie them about thy neck. [22] When thou goest, it shall lead thee; when thou sleepest, it shall keep thee; and when thou awakest, it shall talk with thee. [23] For the commandment is a lamp; and the law is light; and reproofs of instruction are the way of life (KJV).

Prayer

Father God, in the name of Jesus, we thank You for You are an awesome and a powerful God and there is nothing too hard for You. We pull down all strongholds, vain imagination and everything in our lives and in our families that would exult itself about the knowledge of our Lord and Savior, Jesus Christ (2 Corinthians 10:5). We decree and declare that envy, jealousy and strife are severed at the root of conception and shall not bare fruit in our families. We cancel the assignment of the enemy right now to use them to spoil our families. We speak a blessing of peace, love and harmony among our families right now in the name of Jesus. Lord keep us in all our ways and help us to acknowledge You in all our ways as You direct our paths, in Jesus name we pray, Amen.

DAY 45 – HEALING FAMILY RELATIONSHIPS

In a relationships trust is always important. Lying to one another for whatever reason is not advised. The lies you tell today, may surely bite you in the butt tomorrow. If trust is violated one may feel deep pain and wounds to the heart. It could spring from infidelity in a marriage, or our children may violate household rules. Yes it's true that you don't choose your family, but they can usually be trusted to stay in your corner no matter what. When trust is broken, rebuilding trust in your family can be difficult and painful. You may not want to open up your heart to be wounded again, but trust God to see you through. We know that God is a healer and He can heal anything, even a wounded relationship.

So how do we heal and maintain healthy relationships? One of the first things is to start with honesty. When there are issues or problems, discuss them, then seek God's wisdom for resolution. Don't hide or cover over and make excuses for one another, deal with issues directly. Sometimes we just need to hear our mates and children's concerns. A listening ear can go a long way toward understanding how someone else feels. Be slow to speak. Sometimes we just need to cool off when things are heated so that we think more clearly. And then there are times when we just need to let things go. We can't always have our way. If we take the focus off of ourselves and place it on

God especially when all parties are willing to do the same, often times there is quick resolution to issues and restoration of peace. (For more on relationship healing, go back and review day # 44 Jealousy, Envy, Strife: Don't Let Them Spoil Your Family).

2 Chronicles 7:14 [14] If my people, which are called by my name, shall humble themselves, and pray, and seek my face, and turn from their wicked ways; then will I hear from heaven, and will forgive their sin, and will heal their land (KJV).

James 1:19 [19] Wherefore, my beloved brethren, let every man be swift to hear, slow to speak, slow to wrath: (KJV).

Prayer

Lord God Almighty, in the name of Jesus, You're an on time God and awesome in all Your ways. You're a healer and a restorer, full of wisdom and knowledge. You said that we should treat others as we would desire to be treated. In relationships with our families, sometimes we have been self-centered believing everything was all about us at their expense. Father we repent right now for our self-centered behavior and all of our sinfulness and ask You to cleanse us Lord. We ask You to forgive our wicked ways, help us to humble ourselves and seek Your face, in the name of Jesus. Then You will forgive us and repair and heal our broken relationships in Jesus name. Help us to treat each other with care, patience and long suffering. Transform our old ways, bless us with temperance, which is self-control and teach us how to maintain healthy family relationships, in Jesus name. Gracious Lord, thank you for mending and healing our families, Amen.

DAY 46 – FORGIVING FAMILY MEMBERS

The world that we live in today is much more cruel and violent than when we were children. Unfortunately many attacks of violence, physical, verbal and sometimes sexual abuse will come from a family member. God didn't call us to be someone's punching bag or made to feel like a rug or carpet that you walk on daily. He did however, call us to be ones who forgive, yes even our family members.

Matthew 6:12 [12] And forgive us our debts, as we forgive our debtors (KJV).

Luke 6:37 [37] Judge not, and ye shall not be judged: condemn not, and ye shall not be condemned: forgive, and ye shall be forgiven: (KJV).

Prayer

Precious Lord, in the name of Jesus, You are a good, kind and loving Lord. You have called me to love and not to hate, to forgive and not harbor un-forgiveness in my heart. Forgive me Lord for holding on to the hurt and the pain, forgive me for hating them for the evil things that members of my family once did to me. I choose not to judge them, but to cast my cares, my burdens and all old wounds and pain to you Jesus. Lord help me to forgive them as I desire to do and help me love them once again as You do, in Jesus name I ask and pray, Amen.

DAY 47 – LAUGH WITH YOUR FAMILY

Today's Headlines: *100 Year Old Man Father's a Son*

If that was the headlines of your local newspaper today, you might be amazed and you may even laugh. It actually is a truth that is recorded in the bible. It was one of the blessings of Abraham. The Lord God who is so faithful to His every promise, delivered! Upon the hearing of the good news both Abraham and Sarah laughed, Sarah even said the people who would hear about it would laugh with her. Wouldn't it be great if we especially in our families would learn to laugh together with each other and not at one another? The Lord said that we would laugh even in famine (Job 5:22). Laughter is good for the soul. Laughter makes the heart merry (Proverbs 15:13).

Don't laugh at others expense. Don't announce an embarrassing or shameful moment, and do not belittle a family member before a crowd, just to get others to laugh. Words can cut and wound and hurt. Apologies are well advised, but realize words that hurt often get replayed and revisited in our minds over shadowing apologies. Sometimes it's difficult to believe the (positive) kind and encouraging words when many negative words preceded them.

Genesis 17:15-17 [15] And God said unto Abraham, As for Sarai thy wife, thou shalt not call her name Sarai, but Sarah shall her name be. [16] And I will bless her, and give thee a son also of her: yea, I will bless her, and she shall be a mother of nations; kings of people shall be of her. [17] Then Abraham fell upon his face, and laughed, and said in his heart, Shall a child be born unto him that is an hundred years old? and shall Sarah, that is ninety years old, bear (KJV)?

Genesis 18:9-15 [9] "Where is your wife Sarah?" they asked him. "There, in the tent," he said. [10] Then one of them said, "I will surely return to you about this time next year, and Sarah your wife will have a son." Now Sarah was listening at the entrance to the tent, which was behind him. [11] Abraham and Sarah were already very old, and Sarah was past the age of childbearing. [12] So Sarah laughed to herself as she thought, "After I am worn out and my lord is old, will I now have this pleasure?" [13] Then the LORD said to Abraham, "Why did Sarah laugh and say, 'Will I really have a child, now that I am old?' [14] Is anything too hard for the LORD? I will return to you at the appointed time next year, and Sarah will have a son." [15] Sarah was afraid, so she lied and said, "I did not laugh." But he said, "Yes, you did laugh (NIV)."

Genesis 21:1-2, 6-7 [1] Now the LORD was gracious to Sarah as he had said, and the LORD did for Sarah what he had promised. [2] Sarah became pregnant and bore a son to Abraham in his old age, at the very time God had promised him. [6] Sarah said, "God has brought me laughter, and everyone who hears about this will laugh with me." [7] And she added, "Who would have said to Abraham that Sarah would nurse children? Yet I have borne him a son in his old age (NIV)."

Prayer

God of Laughter, God of Compassion, God of Relief, God of Love, in the name of Jesus, I bless Your name. Lord forgive us for the times when we took advantage of others, especially our family members by embarrassing them and revealing their secrets, just for a laugh. Bless us with laughter which makes the heart merry. Let us laugh with one another and not at each other. Help us to be bearers of good news and counselors who hold words in confidence. Bless us to be trustworthy with those things about others that are entrusted to us. Let us bless others with smiles upon our faces and not frowns. Bless us to be peace bearers and joy givers and laugh our hearts merry, in Jesus name, I pray, Amen. Lord thank You for the gift of laughter.

DAY 48 – PRAYING FOR OUR LOVE ONES IN JAILS AND PRISONS

Deliverance is in the House of the Lord. There are times when we go against the will of God and the rules of man that will land us in places where we do not desire to be. Because there are consequences to our actions, when we break the law and are caught, we may find ourselves in jails and prisons. Sometimes that's going to be a physical prison, but then there are other times when that is going to be an emotional, mental or spiritual prison. The good news is that Jesus came to set us free and none of us have to be or remain in prison. Even the one who is in a jailhouse can be free. Oh yes, he may have to complete the serving of his/her time for the consequences of his actions, but may be free in all other ways and be blessed with the salvation and the peace of the Lord. Strongholds do fall and crumble and become ashes under our feet when the Lord delivers us. But we have got to desire to be delivered and turn and change from our evil ways. When we turn it over in faith, the Lord will surely deliver us. The Lord is not ashamed of us, so if we are or family members have been incarcerated, let us not be ashamed of our family members or ourselves. But let us pray with vigor for deliverance and watch the Lord Jesus deliver us/them to freedom.

Psalm 146:7 [7]He uphold the cause of the oppressed and gives food to the hungry, The Lord set prisoners free (NIV).

Isaiah 61:1 ¹The Spirit of the Sovereign Lord is on me, because the Lord has anointed me to proclaim good news to the poor, He has sent me to bind up the brokenhearted, to proclaim freedom for the captives and release from darkness for the prisoners (NIV).

Luke 4:18 ¹⁸ "The Spirit of the Lord is upon me, because he has anointed me to proclaim good news to the poor. He has sent me to proclaim liberty to the captives and recovering of sight to the blind, to set at liberty those who are oppressed (ESV).

John 8:31-32 ³¹....." If you hold to my teaching, you are really my disciples. ³²Then you will know the truth, and the truth will set you free (NIV)."

Galatians 5:1 ¹It is for freedom that Christ has set us free. Stand firm, then and do not let yourselves be burdened again by a yoke of slavery (NIV).

Prayer

The Lord who set us free, our Deliverer, our Way Maker, our Strong Tower, our Burden Bearer, oh Lord we bless You, we praise You, we magnify You, we give You glory and we give You thanksgiving. In the name of Your Son Jesus we bless You with the fruit of our lips. This day we ask You to forgive us for not praying for and visiting our family members who are in jails and prisons. Forgive us for giving up on them Lord, in Jesus name. You said there is a time and season for everything under Heaven. You said there is a time to love and a time to hate. Bless us to not hate them Lord, but hate the actions that resulted in their being imprisoned and jailed. Have mercy upon them Lord, deliver them and set them free. Draw them away from darkness into Your marvelous light. Bless them to be completely delivered this time Lord. Bless them not to be repeat offenders, bless this to be their time of deliverance. Set them free and make them whole. Lord You have given us the power to pull down strongholds and everything that exalts itself above the knowledge of The Most High God. Lord we pull down every stronghold, every vain imagination, every high place and high thing that has lifted itself above the knowledge of God in Jesus name. Lord we bless You and thank You for this being their season of deliverance. Lastly, Lord, for all who are in bondage mentally, spiritually and emotionally, we pull down every stronghold in their lives. We ask You today to break every chain, every shackle and snare, destroy every yoke of bondage. Set them free and make them whole and complete in Jesus name. To God be the glory for all that He has done and for all that He shall yet do, Amen.

DAY 49 – OVERCOMING GRIEF, PRAYING FOR BEREAVED FAMILIES

There is a time and a season for everything under heaven (Ecclesiastes 3:1). There are times when our loved ones will die. If we just keep on living we will all have this experience. The cycle of life continues to turn, we are born and then there is that time in the middle, and then we die. One day we will lose a family member who is close to us and at another time, it may be one that we don't know very well or may have never met. Let God use you as a comforter, for one day you are going to need to be comforted. Be present and spend time with those who are dying, it's called the Ministry of Presence. Don't let your loved ones die alone, bury the old hatchets, let go of un-forgiveness and show God's unconditional love. When you visit the bereaved be a good listener, many times we will not know what to say or we may say the wrong thing and be insensitive. So follow the word and rejoice with those who rejoice and morn with those who morn. Don't forget about them after the funeral, but continue to check in with them, until their joy is restored, for weeping may endure for a night, but joy comes in the morning.

> **Ecclesiastes 3:1-4** [1]To every thing there is a season, and a time to every purpose under the heaven: [2]A time to be born, and a time to die; a time to plant, and a time to pluck up that which is planted; [3]A time to kill, and a time to heal; a time to break down, and a time to build up; [4]A time to weep, and a time to laugh; a time to mourn, and a time to dance (KJV).

1 Thessalonians 4:13-14 [13] But I would not have you to be ignorant, brethren, concerning them which are asleep, that ye sorrow not, even as others which have no hope. [14] For if we believe that Jesus died and rose again, even so them also which sleep in Jesus will God bring with him (KJV).

Romans 12:15 [15] Rejoice with them that do rejoice, and weep with them that weep (KJV).

Prayer

Lord God, my/our Comforter, the One who saw my/our weeping and dried my/ our tears and replaced them with joy. Bless You Lord for comforting and show- ing compassion to all grieving families, including my own. Thank You for heal- ing the brokenhearted and saving those who are crushed in spirit. Thank You for binding up old wounds and healing my/our soul. Thank You for taking up my/ our infirmities, my/our every weakness and carrying all my/our sorrows, every- thing that would ever wound my/our spirit and my/our soul. Bless You for being the Lord of both the living and the dead. I/we trust that my/our love one is at home with You Lord. My/Our soul within me/us is no longer downcast because my/our hope is in You. My/Our season of weeping has ended for You Lord have restored my/our joy. The one/s who once wept, now rejoices and has no more sorrow. My/Our wailing has birthed my/our dance, You have clothed me/us with joy and I/we laugh as my/our heart sings. Thank You and bless You, for You are the Lord of the Dance, the One who has lifted my/our soul. Bless all bereaved families Lord, restore their joy and bless their souls, in Jesus name, Amen.

PRAYER TARGETS AND PERSONAL NOTES

_____
_____
_____
_____
_____
_____
_____
_____
_____
_____
_____
_____
_____
_____
_____
_____
_____
_____
_____
_____
_____
_____
_____
_____
_____
_____
_____
_____

_____
_____
_____
_____
_____
_____
_____
_____
_____
_____
_____
_____
_____
_____
_____
_____
_____
_____
_____
_____
_____
_____
_____
_____
_____
_____
_____
_____

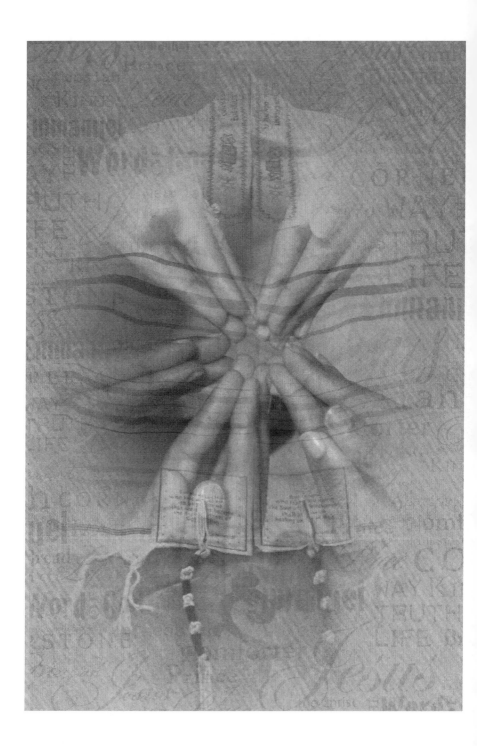

SECTION VII

THANKSGIVING & PRAISE

DAY 50 – A DAY OF PRAISE & THANKSGIVING

Throughout these 50 days there have been many blessings and awesome praise reports. Let's take today to thank God for just being God. Then thank Him for all that He has done and what He is yet doing. Know and believe He is not through with you yet! Praise Him and bless His name!

Psalm 100:4-5 ⁴Enter into his gates with thanksgiving, and into his courts with praise: be thankful unto him, and bless his name. ⁵For the LORD is good; his mercy is everlasting; and his truth endureth to all generations (KJV).

Psalm 103:1-5 ¹Bless the LORD, O my soul: and all that is within me, bless his holy name. ²Bless the LORD, O my soul, and forget not all his benefits: ³Who forgiveth all thine iniquities; who healeth all thy diseases; ⁴Who redeemeth thy life from destruction; who crowneth thee with lovingkindness and tender mercies; ⁵Who satisfieth thy mouth with good things; so that thy youth is renewed like the eagle's (KJV).

`Prayer

El Shaddai, Lord God Almighty, in the name of Jesus, Lord I bless Your holy name. Praise and Glory to my Lord and Savior, Jesus Christ, Lover of my soul, the One who first loved me, who saved my life from destruction and has crowned me with loving kindness. Lord I enter Your gates with thanksgiving and Your courts with praise. Your name is greater than all other names. You are the Alpha and the Omega, the Beginning and the End. You are the great I AM and You have everything that I need. Everything that I need is found in You. You are my Peace, my Joy, my Provider, Jehovah Jireh, my Healer, Jehovah Raphe, my Strength, my Zeal, my Mercy and my Grace. You are the good Sheppard, Jehovah Rohi who came to see about me. There is none greater then You. I thank You Lord for caring for me and about me. I thank You for setting me free and placing my feet on solid ground and the right path that only leads to You, thank You Jesus, Amen.

Prayer of Thanksgiving from *God's Unchanging Hands* 2009

Psalm 119:29 [29]O give thanks unto the LORD; for he is good: for his mercy endureth for ever (KJV).

1 Thessalonians 5:18 [18]Give thanks in all circumstances, for this is God's will for you in Christ Jesus (NIV).

In this season let us give thanks to the Lord for all of His bountiful blessings and for all of His mighty benefits. He has blessed us with our health, strength and wealth and is passing His blessings on to our offspring for generations to come. We thank You for it Lord.

Thank You Lord for Your mercy, Your grace, Your Love and for Your uncommon favor: it endures throughout our lifetime and the lifetime of our seed. We are blessed going in and blessed coming out (Deuteronomy 28:6). You remove darkness from our lives and replace it with light and everlasting life. You have bound death and sent it back to its origins, the evil one. You have made us the salt of the Earth and removed our goat skin and replaced it with lamb's wool. You have removed our stony hearts and replaced them with clean and contrite hearts.

We give thanks to You Lord for Your goodness and Your mercy last forever. We thank You Lord for all that You have done, for all that You are doing and all that You are going to do. You remember not the sins of our youth and our rebellious ways, but according to Your great love, You remember us (Psalm 25:7).

You have given us salvation for free, though it is undeserved. Your Son, our Lord and Savior Jesus Christ died for us on Calvary and covered our sins with His precious flow. You have stayed the hand of the enemy so no weapon formed against us can prosper (Isaiah 54:17). With Your mighty hand with us, who can be against us (Romans 8:31)?

And so we rise to give You praise, we bow before You to honor You and we kneel and humble ourselves before You. We were bought for a high price and can never repay You. In all things we give You thanks. In Jesus name we pray. Amen.

PRAYER TARGETS AND PERSONAL NOTES

_____

_____

_____

_____

_____

_____

_____

_____

_____

_____

_____

_____

_____

_____

_____

_____

_____

_____

_____

_____

_____

_____

_____

_____

_____

_____

_____

_____

_____

_____

_____

_____

FROM THE AUTHOR

I pray you have been blessed as you have traveled this 50 day prayer journey with us. Truly our EMI Missionary Department, EMI Evangelism and Outreach Department, and our EMI Prayer-line partners have been blessed by your joining us in intercession for our families. May God bless you all richly and reward you for your sacrifice.

If you would like to be a blessing to Empowered Ministries, Inc. Evangelism and Outreach Department to keep the word of God and the love of God flowing throughout the Earth, then make your check/s payable to Empowered Ministries, Inc. and place Evangelism and Outreach in the memo section, forward to P. O. Box 4830, 9201 Edgeworth Drive, Capitol Heights, MD 20790-9201 or go to www.empoweredministries.org and click on make a gift. God bless you for your giving.

Lastly, I invite you to join us for our Empowered Ministries, Inc. International Prayer Conference June 6-8, 2014 and our EMI Prayer Retreat June 8-10, 2014. Our theme is "And When We Pray" (Matthew 6:5). Join us in Landover, Maryland for the conference and in the Shenandoah Valley of Virginia for our retreat. Registration is free. Email moniebroadus@gmail.com for more information and so that we can reserve a place for you.

Made in the USA
Charleston, SC
09 March 2014